$2.95X

THE POETICAL WORKS OF
EDWARD TAYLOR

THE
POETICAL
WORKS
OF
EDWARD
TAYLOR

Edited with an Introduction and Notes by

THOMAS H. JOHNSON

PRINCETON UNIVERSITY PRESS

COPYRIGHT 1939 BY ROCKLAND EDITIONS · NEW YORK

Copyright 1943, © 1971 by Princeton University Press

L.C. Card: A45-4662

ISBN 0-691-01275-X

First Princeton Paperback Printing, 1966

Fourth Printing, 1974

This book is sold subject to the condition that it shall not, by way of trade, be lent, resold, hired out, or otherwise disposed of without the publisher's consent, in any form of binding or cover other than that in which it is published.

PRINTED IN THE UNITED STATES OF AMERICA

PRINCETON UNIVERSITY PRESS, PRINCETON, NEW JERSEY

CONTENTS

GODS DETERMINATIONS *(continued)*

SACRAMENTAL MEDITATIONS *(continued)*

SACRAMENTAL MEDITATIONS
SECOND SERIES

FOREWORD TO THE PAPERBACK EDITION

When this volume first appeared, Taylor was virtually unknown. In the intervening years he has taken rank as America's most distinguished poet of the colonial period, and no anthology of American literature fails to represent him. Indeed it is no exaggeration to say that the twentieth-century reassessment of Puritanism, especially in those aspects which reveal the Puritan's feeling for beauty in his hungry search for Heaven, has been given impetus by the appearance of Taylor's poetry.

Taylor designated the verses he composed before his approach to the Lord's Supper *Preparatory Meditations.* On the same manuscript his grandson Ezra Stiles preceded that title with *Sacramental Meditations.* This reprinting continues to use the Stiles' redaction.

T.H.J.

10 November 1965

Lawrenceville, New Jersey

FOREWORD

IT DOES not seem necessary to offer a defense for presenting selections from the "Poetical Works" of Edward Taylor. The verses themselves of this hitherto unknown colonial American poet have merit enough to carry the volume. The sequence of *Gods Determinations* is a well sustained unit, and thus is published entire. The five short poems are unusual prosodic examples, unlike any other verse written by Taylor's New England contemporaries. Some selection from among the two hundred and seventeen *Sacramental Meditations* became necessary, lest the volume be swollen beyond all reasonable bounds. The thirty-two that are chosen seem to be among the best, and adequately represent the quality of all. They have been picked with an eye to displaying the essential nature of Taylor's thought and expression. Of the remaining *poemata,* none seemed of sufficient importance to merit inclusion.

In preparing the text from manuscript, the first consideration has been given to such transcription as accurately represents what Taylor wrote. Spelling, capitalization, and line-spacings follow Taylor exactly, and the few deviations that have been made are recorded in the notes. Intimate acquaintance with Taylor's handwriting has only served to increase the doubt regarding his use of capital "s"; it merges so imperceptibly into the small that some discretion has been necessary. The reader might find grounds for arguing that every "s" used is a capital.

At the same time, no useful purpose can be served by transcribing manuscript peculiarities that are merely "quaint" to the modern eye or ear, and really no part of any "flavor" that Taylor intended. To avoid them therefore, the following changes have been consistently adopted. All manuscript abbreviations have been expanded: *ye* becomes *the; ym, them; &, and; thô, though; m̃, mm; wch, which; chh, church;* etc. The long "s" is shortened; the double "f," intended as a capital, is capitalized; and the modern equivalents for the initial "v" meaning "u," or the internal "u" meaning "v," have been uniformly adopted. In two or three instances quotation marks, never used by Taylor, have been added to avoid confusion. In one respect only has liberty been taken, and that very sparingly. Seventeenth-century punctuation differs so markedly from present day usage that the modern reader is sometimes confused. Taylor, for instance, invariably separated by commas such word pairs as "tall and short," "here and there." The comma for such pairs has not been retained in the printed text. But wherever his thought is clear, or wherever the punctuation or its absence produces an emphasis that may have been intended, no change is made. On the whole, Taylor punctuated carefully, and the changes are confined to obvious needs.

It would have been impossible to publish Taylor's poetry without the gracious permission of Mr. Andrew Keogh, formerly librarian of Yale University, and the cordial aid of the library staff. Lewis S. Gannett, Esquire, of New York City, entrusted to the editor the manuscripts of Taylor that have come into his possession by lineal descent, and Mr. Harold T. Dougherty, librarian of the Westfield Athenaeum, most willingly made available the Taylor manuscripts deposited in the Westfield library. Without such liberality, certain useful data must necessarily have gone unnoticed. The task of establishing such scant biographical information as can be collected would have been impossible without the ready cooperation of Taylor's descendants, who have uniformly aided by volunteering their help. No portrait of Taylor is known to exist, nor is it likely that one was ever made.

Dr. Cyril C. Richardson of Union Theological Seminary obligingly read the portions of the introduction and appendices which attempt to illuminate the theological terms used by Taylor. Professor Stanley T. Williams most generously consented to read the manuscript, and his excellent suggestions clarified several points. The editor's debt to Professor Donald F. Cameron and Dr. Allan V. Heely is one that cannot easily be repaid. Their learning and sound good sense preserved him from innumerable errors of fact and procedure. To Professor Austin Warren and Professor Perry Miller the indebtedness is immense. They have been in touch with the undertaking from the first, and their scholarship, wisdom, and taste have supplied many a deficiency which would otherwise have been glaringly apparent.

T. H. J.

5 February 1939
Lawrenceville, New Jersey

EDWARD TAYLOR

T SEEMS probable that had the poetry of Edward Taylor been published during his lifetime, he would long since have taken a place among the major figures of colonial American literature. It is startling at so late a period to run upon him. Edward Taylor was an orthodox Puritan minister, who lived nearly sixty years in the frontier village of Westfield, Massachusetts, writing poetry until 1725 in the mannered style of the pre-restoration sacred poets. Though no imitator, he was really in the tradition of Donne and the Anglo-Catholic conceitists. His sole inspiration was a glowing, passionate love for Christ, expressed in terms of his own unworthiness and wistful yearning. However much the substance of his imagination was erected within the frame of a special theology, his vitality as a prosodist and his evident delight in tone and color indicate how thoroughly he enjoyed poetry as an art. It is questionable, indeed, whether the depth of his poetic imagination and the vigor of his inventive fancy were equaled in verse by any of his countrymen until the nineteenth century. Only the fact that he "gave orders that his heirs should never publish any of his writings"[1] can account for the obscurity into which his verses were consigned. The injunction happily is no longer in effect, and the "Poetical Works" can now be examined.[2]

Little is to be discovered about Taylor from any published record, yet there must have been qualities especially winning in his nature, if we may judge by the welcome which he received from discerning gentlemen when he disembarked at Boston, early in July, 1668. The first day or two after his passage from England, his diary records, he spent as guest of Increase Mather, even at that early date one of the leading ministers of the town, and himself but recently returned from a sojourn abroad. Taylor had come to him with letters of introduction, to be sure, but had come as a youth of twenty-two or twenty-three, with no evident background of position or accomplishment. The young man must very soon have become an intimate of the Mather family, for years later, when Taylor wrote an elegy on the death of Increase,[3] he recalled how

> Nigh Sixty years ago I wept in verse
> When on my Shoulders lay thy Fathers herse.

The gracious reception of the Mathers gave Taylor breathing space, and doubtless helped him along. Very shortly, with more letters, he presented his duties to John Hull, the mint-master and the wealthiest New Englander of his day. Hull warmed to the personable exile, for he would not hear of Taylor's departure for a full week. It seems to have been in the hope of graduating from college and entering the ministry that the ardent young Congregationalist had left England, at that time a country which did not favor gentlemen of quick parts who vigorously advocated civil and religious liberty. But the Bay colonists were glad to receive him, and his aspirations were probably encouraged by Mather and Hull, for on the fourteenth Taylor journeyed to Cambridge, and called upon the president of Harvard. Mr. Chauncy interviewed him, and insisted upon his spending the night. Taylor stayed, sharing a chamber with the President's son Elnathan. The conference with President Chauncy terminated satisfactorily, for Taylor was immediately admitted to the class of 1671. He was thus closely associated with Increase Mather's nephew Samuel, and with one who shortly became his good friend and roommate, Samuel Sewall. Years later, in looking back upon his friendship with Taylor, Sewall recalled that "He and I were Chamber fellows and Bed-fellows in Harvard-College Two years: He being admitted into the College, drew me thither."[1] Clearly Taylor had that within, which captivated those who came to know him.

No available sources give an adequate picture of the Taylor family. Edward Taylor's diary, kept during the tedious six-weeks' voyage, mentions a brother Richard whom he left in England. In 1691, by the death of a sister's only child, William Arms, he inherited land in Virginia,[2] but no other clues appear. He was born in Coventry, or perhaps in the hamlet of Sketchley, not far away in the neighboring county of Leicestershire. Quite evidently the family were dissenters, and Ezra Stiles, Taylor's grandson, had it on family tradition that his grandfather was determined to leave England, after the persecutions of 1662, for liberty of conscience. He had delayed his departure for some reason not stated, teaching school at Bagworth, and thus when he entered Harvard he was two or three years older than any of his ten classmates.

Taylor's undergraduate life was passed uneventfully. For two of the three and a half years during his residence he served as student butler, an office which devolved upon a sober, responsible undergraduate, usually somewhat older than his classmates. In May of his senior year he was one of four chosen to declaim in the College Hall before the President and fellows.[1] The youthful poetaster chose to praise the superiority of English over Hebrew and the classic languages, but he had not then developed the imaginative apprehension of form and color which he later displays. Instead, he piled conceits together with labored ingenuity.

> Let English then to finde its Worth be presst
> Unto the touch of Generalls Speeches test.
> Speech is the Chrystall Chariot where the minde
> In progress rides, Cart rutting of the Winde:
> Whose Coachman drives Coach and Coach horses there
> Rattling along the Mouth in at the eare. . . .

One hopes that the aged President Chauncy listened to the thirty-minute declamation with kindly forbearance!

At the time of Taylor's graduation, the frontier settlement of Westfield, lying some hundred miles southwest of Boston on the other side of the Connecticut River, sent a call to Harvard for a promising young minister: the twelve or fifteen church members wished to organize under their own pastor. Westfield was less isolated than its scant population would indicate, for it lay on the northern border of Connecticut, and was near other well settled communities. Taylor seems to have been the only member of the graduating class who was pressed to accept the offer. He decided to do so, and set out for Westfield, a young bachelor, early in December, 1671. Though his ordination was delayed eight years by King Philip's War, the town voted at the end of the first year to settle him.[2] Having thus finally established himself, Taylor next looked about for a suitable wife, and his choice fell upon Elizabeth Fitch, a daughter of the pastor in Norwich, Connecticut. Of the seven children born to them between 1675 and 1688, none outlived their father. Elizabeth died just a year after the birth of her last child. In 1692, Taylor married a daughter of the Hon. Samuel Wyllys of Hartford, who survived her husband by a few months. All six children of this marriage lived to maturity and established families of their own, though only one son, born of this second marriage, lived to perpetuate the family name.

The afflictions that beset the minister's household were perhaps no more severe than those which visited any seventeenth-century family, where childbirth fever claimed many mothers, and the scourge of smallpox and wasting terrors of consumption were dread threats. One can imagine the dismay which gripped Sewall when he learned, probably from the captain of a trading vessel, of the death of young James Taylor, the twenty-two year old son of his close friend. On him fell the task of breaking the news to the father. The young man had gone to the West Indies late in the year 1700 to sell horses shipped from Boston. Sewall softened the blow with what sympathy he could give. He wrote Taylor that James, having arrived at Barbados on the eighteenth of January, 1701, fell sick of a fever, died within a week, and was buried on the island. "My wife and I more than sympathize with you, the Loss is partly our own."[1] As one reads Taylor's poem "On Wedlock and the Death of Children," written some years before, with its yearning love for the broken "branches" already taken from him, and its willing surrender of them to Christ, one knows what this later blow must have cost him. But nothing represents the staunchness of his character better than the gallant verses which he penned on the day of his wife's death.[2] Their restraint is ennobled by the complete assurance of her salvation, and his own Christian hope of reunion.

> Lord, arke my Soule safe in thyselfe, whereby
> I and my Life again may joyned bee.

The Meditation is fired with a delicate animation entirely lacking in the formal elegy which he composed a few days later to commemorate the passing of this thirty-eight year old wife, who had died "at night about two hours after Sun setting."[3] In none of his poems is there a hint of bitterness over his losses. The serenity of his faith was complete.

Taylor lived a life of quiet usefulness in Westfield for fifty-eight years, serving both as pastor and physician to his flock. It was an "Angelical Conjunction," as Cotton Mather had once termed it,[4] practiced by many colonial ministers in the early period of the New England settlements. There were the annual ministers' meetings to attend, now in one town, now in another, and an occasional horseback trip to a Harvard commencement. In 1720, when Taylor was approaching seventy-five, his alma mater conferred a master's degree upon him. Beyond the record of such events, very few contemporary glimpses have been handed down to enliven the portrait of the man. His grandson Stiles was too young to remember the aged gentleman who passed quietly away in 1729, "entirely enfeebled, ... longing and waiting for his Dismission."[1] Yet Stiles of course knew about him, and set down what he had heard: that his grandfather had been "A man of small stature but firm: of quick Passions—yet serious and grave."[2] Indeed, the characterization was apt, and Sewall illuminates Taylor's persuasiveness with one revealing flash: "I have heard him preach a Sermon at the Old South [Church] upon short warning which as the phrase in England is, might have been preached at Paul's Cross."[3]

During the last three years of his life Taylor was assisted in his pastoral duties by the Reverend Mr. Nehemiah Bull, a young graduate of Yale, who succeeded him as minister; it was he no doubt who wrote the obituary that appeared with a Westfield date-line in the *Boston News-Letter* of August 14, 1729. By will Taylor left a library of some two hundred volumes, which for the most part went to Stiles. The small personal estate of a few hundred pounds must have been soon disbursed, for out of it, Stiles says, "Uncle Eldad [Taylor's only surviving son] paid £700 Debts" contracted by Taylor: "most[ly] at Boston for Daughters Setting out."[4] It is not surprising. There were four of them, all married between 1720 and 1722, to coming young ministers. The tombstone marking his grave is still preserved in the old Westfield burying ground, recalling that the "Aged, Venerable, Learned, & Pious Pastor . . . Serued God and his Generation Faithfully for Many Years."

HIS POETRY

A LL OF Taylor's verses are bound between the covers of a four-hundred-page manuscript volume. Aside from a few conventional *threnodia* and a half dozen short lyrics, the "Poetical Works" comprises but two general groups of any consequence: *Gods Determinations* and the *Sacramental Meditations,* both shortly to be discussed. Surveying the poetry as a whole, one is struck by Taylor's inventiveness. He plays upon the language as if it were an instrument, and the boldness of his figures allies him with the poets of the late Elizabethan period, rather than with those of his own day. Even in his choice of unusual metrical patterns he adheres to earlier fashions. He secures an effective variety in the closely knit sequences of *Gods Determinations* by using twelve metrical forms, some of them "Pindarics" without precise counterpart; and only one, the decasyllabic couplet, at all commonly found in English poetry. His six-line iambic pentameter stanza riming ababcc in the *Meditations* has the advantage of supplying a leisurely vehicle for the narrative passages, while at the same time conveying a noble serenity to the lyric outbursts.

The ardor of Taylor's love for Christ is displayed best in the songs which conclude *Gods Determinations* and in the *Meditations,* but the reader need not search afield for analogues among the verses of the seventeenth-century conceitists to explain Taylor's choice of subject. It is true that the manner and devices of his poems especially suggest the example of George Herbert, the Anglican poet beloved so much by Puritans. Five of the unusual metrical patterns of *Gods Determinations* exactly correspond to forms in Herbert's *The Temple.* There are, too, the same rhetorical devices of question, refrain, apostrophe, and direct address. There is an observable correspondence in the length of their songs, and it is further apparent that Taylor believes with Herbert that nothing is so mean but that it can be ennobled by figures from common life, from medical and chemical knowledge. He likewise draws heavily upon metaphors of taste, smell, color, and sound. But there are qualities as well in the verse which ally him more closely with Richard Crashaw than with Herbert: the moods of seraphic exaltation, in which the language of amorous poetry is adapted to religious ends; the prodigality of fanciful tropes; and the complete, almost physical, abandonment to Christ. Yet clearly Taylor does not merely imitate. He was possibly not conscious of the similarities, and in fact is unlikely to have read a line of Crashaw's poetry.

The spirit which animated Taylor's devotion was fully as central in Puritan as in Anglican or Catholic thought. Within Puritanism itself, though not often displayed in verse, is to be discovered all the spiritual fervor that found utterance in his poems. His intense love for Christ supplied the matter; delight in conceits, somewhat belated in point of time, determined the manner. Taylor's debt to other poets, if debt there be, is less obvious. One thinks naturally of Quarles, the laureate among Puritans, whose *Emblemes,* starting from some text of Scripture on which he finds a meditation, may well have furnished a model for the *Sacramental Meditations.*[1] One would like to know whether a copy of Sir John Davies's *Nosce Teipsum* may not have passed through Taylor's hands. Davies's combination of poetry and metaphysics, his discourses on the longing, grief, and destiny of the soul, somewhat parallel *Gods Determinations* and certain of the *Meditations.* No suggestion of the influence of Wither, so often the Puritan's inspiration, is anywhere apparent. On the whole, one's impression is that Taylor struck out for himself. The wealth of colloquial, indigenous terms, adopted from the language of everyday life, often recalled from the technical phrases used by the weavers of his native Warwickshire, produces an effect, when combined with the vigor of his thought and the sensitivity of his ear, that leaves no doubt of his originality. Taylor's delight in the sound and shading of language, a further Elizabethan characteristic, is emphasized by his word coinages: there seems to be no recorded example to match substantives like "squitchen," "glore," "reech," "pillard," and "hone."[2]

The *Meditations* lack the stanzaic variety of *Gods Determinations* in that they uniformly employ the six-line stanza. Their diction, like that found in the lines of the "conceitists" generally, is partly learned and Latinic, partly homely. The lines are concentrated and angular, sometimes rough: an inevitable tendency of verse called metaphysical, wherein the conceit is inspired by a philosophical concept. But at his best Taylor achieves a striking unity of design by developing one figure. He is always the object through which Christ transmits his influence, now as a garden exhaling odor, or as a pipe conveying liquid, or a loom whereon the spirit weaves, or a mint in which God coins his image. By thus developing one single figure in a poem, Taylor avoids a fault to which almost all sacred poets are commonly prone, that is, of strewing metaphors throughout their verses with prodigal abandon. For instance, the figure of Christ as attorney pleading man's cause *sub forma pauperis* before God, the Judge, in Meditation Thirty-Eight, is carefully built up without extraneous imagery. The legal phraseology, so often seized upon to express the covenant idea, is consistently employed and brought to a climax without wrenched or tortured figures. Indeed, it becomes plain by 1685 that Taylor has enriched and deepened his concept of the poetic art to the point where thereafter his *Meditations* are often firmer and sometimes more brilliant statements of his theological position.

Puritans were especially eager to find "types," that is, analogies or correspondent realities between events or persons in the Old Testament and in the New. By such means did they feel that God's word was illuminated and man's emotions stirred. Christ, the antitype, was foreshadowed by whatever prophetic similitude the reader might discover. Thus in a few of the *Meditations* Taylor narrates Old Testament stories as "types" of Christ's advent and suffering, and at moments is able to create striking effects by the speed and concreteness of his narrative summary.[1]

> Jonas did type this thing, who ran away
>   From God and, shipt for Tarsus, fell asleep.
> A Storm lies on the Ship: the Seamen they
>   Bestir their Stumps, and at wits end do weep:
>   'Wake, Jonas:' who saith, 'Heave me over deck;
>   The Storm will Cease then; all lies on my neck.'

Occasionally Taylor composed elegies in frigid decasyllabics.[2] But such "effusions" are not stamped with the image of his personality. In his devotional poetry, on the other hand, he is thoroughly at home, and the fire of that devotion abates very little with the passage of years. His last meditation, written in 1725, when he was past eighty, is as ardent in its expression of love for God as his earlier verses. The text is from Canticles, II: 5: "I am sick of love," and opens with the cry: "Heart sick, my Lord, heart sick of Love to thee."

18

The poet's taste had been formed early, perhaps in Harvard College, perhaps in England before he sailed for Massachusetts Bay; and it never changed. He lived remote from the sources of poetry and from the currents and fashions of a new era. Yet, in view of his exclusive devotion to religious poetry, it is doubtful whether new fashions would have interested him, even supposing he was aware of them. The inventory of his library does not furnish a real clue, for oddly enough it contains only one book of English poetry: Anne Bradstreet's verses. Perhaps the most teasing of all questions that remain unanswered is why he directed his heirs never to publish his verse. Of the many possible answers that suggest themselves, none seems more consistent with the glimpse one catches of his quiet life, his abiding love for his Redeemer, than such as argues a modesty and a sense of human unworthiness that was thorough-going. Taylor seems to have been free from the last infirmity of noble minds.

Of Taylor's contemporaries, one is in the habit of praising "The Tenth Muse" for her charming sincerity, the very local Benjamin Tompson for smoothness, and the well remembered Michael Wigglesworth for historic importance and an occasional stanza of power. The flaws of Taylor's metrics are plain; yet here was a provincial minister and physician who chose poetry the more radiantly to honor the free and boundless mercy of Christ; one who, loving poetry for its own sake, wrote in homely language with a delicacy and brilliance unparalleled in colonial letters.

GODS DETERMINATIONS

I LOVE to Sweeten my mouth with a piece of *Calvin,* before I go to sleep," John Cotton is reported to have said,[1] and in his own day Cotton's remark would have caused no bewilderment. His taste for knotty problems of theology was not the curious whim of an obscure divine, and it is vain to hope for understanding of Puritan literature without realizing that Cotton's predilection was shared by nearly all seventeenth-century gentlemen. Indeed, as we know today, theological dogma, passing through the alembic of Milton's genius, is not unlovely; and in Taylor's verse sequence, dwelling as it does on election, reprobation, free grace, and church fellowship, Puritan doctrine can at times take on a radiant sweetness. Stripped of its specialized theology, Taylor's theme is one that has taxed men's profoundest creative faculties through the ages. It is moral in the sense that all great stories essentially must be, whether written or sung or painted. It is the story of man's struggle to understand himself in his relation to God. The particular "fable" with which Dante or Milton, Wigglesworth or Taylor chooses to clothe a moral truth becomes tedious only when the art of its presentation or the spirit behind its conception fails to convince. Yet none of the four, the great together with the lesser, can be understood until the philosophic pattern is displayed. Taylor, as much as Milton, was writing to justify God's ways to man, but his emphasis is different. He did not purpose to give epic effects to Chaos, Heaven, and Hell, but to justify Covenant theology by way of poetic exposition in highly wrought imagery. The limits that he set himself brings *Gods Determinations* more closely into line with *The Day of Doom* than with *Paradise Lost,* though it is actually quite unlike either. But within the limits, Taylor displays a talent more akin to that of the greater poet for dressing old concepts in memorable language.

To the extent that *Gods Determinations* is written with speaking characters it resembles a morality play, but the speakers develop no dramatic individuality. In all, six are presented: Mercy, Justice, Christ, Satan, the Soul, and a Saint, that is, the "Pious Wise" man, who has experienced reversion to faith. In delineation Satan, even as with Milton, is the most nearly dimensional, though even the shadowy Satan achieves no dramatic entity. The thirty-five sequences have lyric, rather than dramatic, unity, and the seven paeans which conclude the poem move with splendid swiftness to a finish that raises the whole sequence far above mere versified expositions. The color and tone rarely sink into bathos. Taylor carries to his Saviour "wagon-loads" of love; Satan appears with "goggling eyes," inducing sinners as "Jayle Birds" to ride "pick-pack." The metaphoric extravagances seldom strain the reader's sense of the appropriate, and the imagery is drawn from the homely experiences of a pastor and physician; from the world which Taylor knew, not from literary conventions. It is in such characteristics that the charm of Taylor's individuality finds scope.

Gods Determinations opens with a "Preface" celebrating God as the Creator who molded the world, laid its cornerstone, spread its canopies, made its curtain rods, bowled the sun in a cosmic bowling-ally, and above the whole hung the stars as "twinckling Lanthorns."

Man was created, sinned, and thereby lost the world. In the short "Prologue" following, man, a "Crumb of Earth," will glorify this "Might Almighty," and Taylor, breathing a hope that his pen may move aright, invokes God's aid lest his "dull Phancy" stir, not mercy, but scorn. The story begins with a brief account of man's fall, and his consequent fear of divine retribution. Justice and Mercy, seeing the creature "Sculking on his face" fall to debate, in language couched in the legal phraseology so often adopted by Covenant theologians, over the question whether man deserves salvation. Mercy argues that

> Though none are Sav'd that wickedness imbrace,
> Yet none are Damn'd that have Inherent Grace.

He points out that Christ, as scapegoat, took upon himself the sins of mankind, purchasing for the creature His "milkwhite Robe of Lovely Righteousness." But the creature is still crippled by his fall. Mercy pities his infirmity, but realistically concludes that, though man has "broke his Legs, yet's Legs his Stilts must bee." The pity goes further still, for grace will mend the injury, yet man has blindly and foolishly rejected it. Mercy's gift is scorned:

> But most he'l me abuse, I feare, for still
> Some will have Farms to farm, some wives to wed:
> Some beasts to buy; and I must waite their Will.
> Though while they scrape their naile or scratch their head,
> Nay, though with Cap in hand I Wooe them long,
> They'l whistle out their Whistle e're they'l come.

Justice advises that the best way for man to achieve happiness is to obey the moral law, the Ten Commandments; for he can never win salvation on his own merits.

> Whos'ever trust doth, to his golden deed
> Doth rob a barren Garden for a Weed.

But Mercy's plea wins Justice over, for by the terms of the new covenant of grace God's mercy supersedes His justice. Man therefore is bound over to Mercy, who knows that salvation is promised by God to all who have faith in Christ, whose purchase procured man's pardon.

> For Justice nothing to thy Charge can lay;
> Thou hast Acquittance in thy surety.

The significance of the debate and its conclusion is lost on man, who peeps about "With Trembling joynts, and Quivering Lips," aware only of his lapsed estate, fearing the consequences of the compact which he broke.

> Thus man hath lost his Freehold by his ill:
> Now to his Land Lord tenent is at Will,
> And must the Tenement keep in repare,
> Whate're the ruins and the Charges are.

Crippled and footsore, mankind is invited by God to a "mighty sumptuous" repast, and for the journey thither "the Sinfull Sons of men" are provided a royal coach. But most of them regard the feast of graces spread before them as mere "Slobber Sawces." So froward are they in their dullness that they "hiss piety" and scant all graces. Mercy and Justice are angered into a pursuit of men, to bring them to the table by force, but the congregation divides into ranks and flees from God's presence. Soon captured, the "poor souls" sue for pardon, while Satan appears to taunt them. In their despair they address Christ for aid, and his reply cheers them, until Satan, who "Doth winnow them with all his wiles" charges them with apostasy, saying that no hope exists for men so steeped in villainy and sin. In extended debate between Satan and the Soul, both the inward and the outward man are accused of deadly sins. The Soul cries out in agony to Christ again, and is answered with lines that radiate a graciousness so real, so poignantly touching, that the reader cannot fail to experience with Taylor his devout emotion. The ecstasy of joy prompted by Christ's reply brings to an end the part of the poem dealing with the second rank: those who, seriously regenerate, have found salvation by faith.

At this point a third rebellious rank, who have progressed but a short way in their regeneration, come under Satan's lashing sophistry, and are moved to bewail their helplessness in a threnodial dialogue. But even though they fully anticipate eternal death, they look about once more to be comforted by their former champion Mercy, for "If dy we must, in mercy's arms wee'l dy." The Soul is now prepared to receive assistance from one who has truly experienced sanctification; one who is properly regenerate and knows how to sympathize with as well as instruct unregenerate man. In the person of such a "Pious Wise" one, or Saint,[1] the Soul finds help, and with him enters into dialogue. The Saint knows how to resolve the doubts which the Soul raises.

> But muster up your Sins, though more or few:
> Grace hath an Edge to Cut their bonds atwo.

Satan, he explains, is impotent in the face of Christ's limitless grace. Even after we are reborn we tend to revert to our natural state, and such flaws as appear even in saints darken or stain the color of "that thrice Ennobled noble Gem," the Soul:

> Are Flaws in Venice Glasses bad? What in
> Bright Diamonds? What then in man is Sin?

But the grace working in us is the needlework of Providence, sometimes weather beaten, and never fully unrolled. It is therefore not to be judged now, when we would be able to see and understand so little of it. We know only that the grace within *does* work. Above all, the Saint reminds his listener, that

> If in the golden Meshes of this Net,
> (The Checkerwork of Providence) you're Caught,
> And Carri'de hence to Heaven, never fret:
> Your Barke shall to an Happy Bay be brought.

And finally, the Saint advises, lose yourself in contemplation of the happiness which is the end for which God designed his creature. Give over the questioning whether God cares for you.

> Call not in Question whether he delights
> In thee, but make him thy Delight.

It is at this point that the arguments for grace and faith and regeneration in terms of Covenant theology, neatly presented as they have been, give way to an art that raises the poem by a lyrical outburst into a place far beyond anything achieved by Americans until long after Taylor's day. The Soul is now convinced of its sin, the first step in regeneration, and moves rapidly through the stages toward glorification, that final state of felicity which can never be completed on earth. The last seven lyrics, each conceived in a different metrical pattern, animate religious doctrine with creative fire. Though they can stand as authentic lyrics by themselves, viewed as a climax to the whole sequence, their effect is symphonic. The awakening Soul's discovery of its power is uttered timidly at first, but as realization turns to conviction, its cry is triumphantly flung out:

> methinks I soar
> Above the stars, and stand at Heavens Doore.

From this point to the end, the joy of achievement finds glowing expression in the illuminated faith of the poet, set forth with metaphoric brilliance.

SACRAMENTAL MEDITATIONS

W E CANNOT read Taylor's *Sacramental Meditations* without a deep awareness of his overwhelming devotion to Christ's love, and his absorption in the being of his Savior. He expresses himself with autobiographic intimacy. At first we may wonder that a Puritan would abandon himself so fully to a passionate religious exaltation. Such an ardor as he felt may lead the unwary to conclude that Puritans were sacramentalists, or that Taylor was in some degree unorthodox; that somewhere here is displayed an extreme view of the efficacy of the sacraments; the view that the sacraments themselves by Christ's institution confer grace upon the recipient by direct spiritual efficacy. But the truth is otherwise. The *Meditations* need no analogues among Anglo-Catholic sacramentalists to explain their adoration of Christ. At the core of Puritanism, as it was practiced in seventeenth-century New England, are to be found all the humility and all the passionate love for Christ that are necessary.

In common with members of all Christian churches, Puritans observed the sacraments of baptism and the Eucharist, or Lord's Supper, as they preferred to call it. But the seventeenth-century Puritans of New England had an especially compelling reason for assigning to the ordinance of the Lord's Supper an importance which elsewhere it did not always achieve. The foundation of their religious belief was Covenant theology, and of this form Taylor was a thoroughly orthodox exponent. Covenant theology postulated an agreement or compact between God and Adam whereby God freely promised Adam, and through him all his posterity, eternal happiness, providing only that Adam obey God's injunction. But mankind forfeited God's promise when Adam broke the compact, the

Covenant of Works, and thereby were subject to God's wrath and condemnation. Nevertheless, God, of His own free will, instituted a new Covenant of Grace, by which all men were given reason to hope for salvation, on condition only that they believe in Christ. Since it was only through Christ's supreme and willing sacrifice of himself that men could now hope to win eternal bliss, they had therefore an even more compelling reason to live up to the terms of the agreement, and to honor the memory of Christ's death and resurrection. Though the Puritan had no dispute with his Anglican brethren about the meaning of the Lord's Supper, his approach to it was undertaken with full knowledge that for him there was no salvation unless he could actively participate in the humility which he must feel toward himself for the first broken covenant, and could rejoice at the thought that Christ stood sponsor for him in the second. If only he might seal his part of the compact!

Thus it becomes clear that, though the manner in which Puritans observed the ordinance of communion remained strictly Calvinistic, and conformed essentially to that which obtained in the Anglican church, the intensity of their observance was more keenly motivated. To the Puritan, mankind had barely escaped a most terrible damnation solely because God had willingly and with supreme loving-kindness instituted a new covenant. He had designed it entirely for man's happiness, since, as Milton said:

> God doth not need
> Either man's work or his own gifts.

Mankind had forfeited all reasonable expectation of salvation by breaking the terms of the first covenant, and God's sealing of a new one was unparalleled kindness. Throughout, God had treated men with perfect justice, but he had gone still further. Having looked upon men as reasonable creatures from whom he did not expect mere blind obedience, God above all desired their happiness, since they alone of all creatures were able to achieve it. They possessed such stock of inherent grace as, by improvement, could win for them felicity. "What is Vanity," exclaimed Samuel Willard, "but a missing the End?"[1] Thus it was with a heart made especially humble by the immediacy of God's free grace and Christ's boundless love that the Puritan approached the Lord's table.

Except for the exalted place which Puritans gave to the Scriptures, and their covenantal doctrine of man's relation to God, together with certain less central questions of ritual and polity, they were in almost total agreement with the Anglican creed. The emigrations to Massachusetts during the decade of the 1630's were not composed of Separatists, but of Episcopalians fleeing Archbishop Laud's "innovations in religion," since his changes in ritual tended toward Roman practice. In all ways Puritanism had stemmed from Anglicanism, and it therefore recognized in the matter of sacraments only baptism and the Eucharist. On this point both sects were Sacramentarians, that is, opposers of the Roman Catholic doctrine of transubstantiation and the Lutheran theory of consubstantiation. They maintained that Christ ordained those two sacraments and none other, disputing with learned casuistry the Latin doctors who contended that Christ had instituted all seven. The violence which Anglicans felt toward the Roman Catholic doctrine was carried over into the Puritan churches of New England with fierce intensity, and at no point do their objections appear more cogently argued than in their defence of the Lord's Supper.[1] To orthodox Puritans it was explicity not a converting ordinance, though it was a means whereby men were helped to a state of salvation by conversion. There was no "cultism" in their theory of sacraments, nor is there the least indication of any in Taylor's *Meditations*.

The best New England spokesman on these points was Samuel Willard, vice president of Harvard College, and minister of the Old South Church in Boston from 1676 till his death in 1707. Once a month from January 31, 1687/8, until April 1, 1707, Willard gave a series of public lectures on the Assembly's Shorter Catechism, that body of doctrine on which both Puritan and Anglican faith was founded. The fame of Willard's sermons drew large numbers, and a demand for their publication was finally answered by the posthumous issue of a nine-hundred-page folio volume.[2] Its exposition of the ordinance of the Lord's Supper as it was practiced in the Puritan churches establishes the ardor and humility of Taylor's *Meditations* as thorough-going and essentially Puritan qualities. God had made a promise, so the doctrine is expounded, and the sacrament was a seal to the instrument. How invigorating, then, how glorious was the assurance thus given to all participants!

The idea of the seal, as an actual wafer authenticating the royal charter, is stressed both in the general Puritan theory and in Taylor's poetry. The sacrament thus became a writ or warrant, a *sacramentum*, given under the security of God's explicit pledge "to signify the outward Signs and Seals of the New Covenant,"[1] binding both the sovereign and the recipient. To be sure, the terms of the charter did not postulate the sacrament as a converting ordinance: that is, it did not make men Christians. It was a means toward conversion by way of the Word of God, the Scriptures, the principal medium; and to that it was annexed. Its efficacy was confirmed in the Covenant of Grace. At this point the Puritan and Catholic theory of the Eucharist differs centrally, for to the Puritan the operation of the sacrament is moral, not physical or "natural." The bread and wine of the Lord's Supper, the Puritans maintained, was the real spiritual presence of Christ, as Calvin had taught, but it was not the physical Christ. There was no mysterious transubstantiation of the Eucharist into Christ's physical body.[2] The fact that by Roman Catholic doctrine the laity should be denied the wine, which was reserved for the priesthood, seemed blasphemous. Other details of Catholic administration were deemed objectionable: the bread placed in the mouth, rather than the hand; the giving of it unbroken.

The Puritan's constant analysis of his emotions and understanding, his searching of his heart and mind, are well-known characteristics. They were never demanded with more importunity than at the sacred rite of the Lord's Supper. Taylor's *Meditations* but heighten and configure the terms which Willard employs in describing the necessary preparation.

And if none be admitted but such as are Knowing and Orthodox in Principles, make a Profession of Subjection to Christ, and their Conversations are as becometh Christians, or if they have been Scandalous, testify [their] Repentance and Reformation; there will be no blame upon the Churches of Christ who entertain them.

Though men must examine their worthiness and "preparedness," yet its presence does not "at all intend a Personal Merit, . . . for when in a Legal sense we are most sensible of, and affected with our own Unworthiness, we are Evangelically most Worthy; and the word itself properly signifies, *meet for a thing*. . . . And it is certain, that a Man may be Habitually prepared, and yet Actually unprepared, and be very unfit for present Communion in it, and so lose the bene-

fit of it. And the reason of this is, because of the remaining Corrup
tion which in this Life abides in the best of God's People, which
puts a woful impediment to their receiving of Spiritual good by
any Ordinance." Thus the heart must be searched, each man look
ing into his own, "to find enough to humble us, by reason of so
much Corruption that we shall discern to be stirring in us, and so
much Infirmity attending on all our Graces."[1]

With the heart prepared, then, the partaker was ready to experi
ence the chief design of the ordinance, which is to set forth Christ's
love; and the act of eating and drinking gives men "an heart-affect
ing representation of it." Willard's exposition reveals that the Puri
tan emphasis, in administering communion, directed men to expe
rience the ardent intensity of Christ's redeeming love. The very im
ages themselves by which Willard clothes the figure of that love are
so essential to Puritan thought that Taylor's adoption of them in the
Meditations was inevitable. Willard says that those are wrong who
partake unless they believe the benefit comes because of Christ's
"Mediatorial Sufferings, which he suffered in his Humane Nature
to make Satisfaction to offended Justice."

This Ordinance is called a Feast, and Feasts are made for friendship;
which supposeth Love, and that without dissimulation. . . . In a Word,
it is to be a Commemoration of the greatest Love, which cannot be done
as it ought to be, without the reciprocation of our most ardent and in
tense Love. . . . If there be any thing that we love better, or equally with
him, we do not Love him at all. So that tho' there is a Love which we owe
to the Creature, yet when it comes in competition with this, it is compar
atively hatred. . . . If we Love him as we ought, he is our all. . . . If we do
not come to enjoy him, and lie in his Embraces, we do not come with a
right design, nor can we expect to profit.

Thus does Willard make clear[2] that an ardent humility is basic in
Puritan faith. It is that quality precisely which Taylor carried over
into the *Sacramental Meditations;* he but enriched and expanded
the figures. His intensity was shared, though surely not equaled, by
every Puritan partaker of the holy ordinance.

Gods Determinations Touching His Elect:

AND

The Elects Combat In Their Conversion,

AND

Coming Up To God In Christ:

TOGETHER WITH

The Comfortable Effects Thereof

The Preface

Infinity, when all things it beheld,
In Nothing, and of Nothing all did build,
Upon what Base was fixt the Lath, wherein
He turn'd this Globe, and riggalld it so trim?
Who blew the Bellows of his Furnace Vast?
Or held the Mould wherein the world was Cast?
Who laid its Corner Stone? Or whose Command?
Where stand the Pillars upon which it stands?
Who Lac'de and Fillitted the earth so fine,
With Rivers like green Ribbons Smaragdine?
Who made the Sea's its Selvedge, and it locks
Like a Quilt Ball within a Silver Box?
Who Spread its Canopy? Or Curtains Spun?
→ Who in this Bowling Alley bowld the Sun?
Who made it always when it rises set:
To go at once both down, and up to get?
Who th' Curtain rods made for this Tapistry?
Who hung the twinckling Lanthorns in the Sky?[1]
Who? who did this? or who is he? Why, know
It's Onely Might Almighty this did doe.
His hand hath made this noble worke which Stands
His Glorious Handywork not made by hands.
Who spake all things from nothing; and with ease
Can speake all things to nothing, if he please.
Whose Little finger at his pleasure Can
Out mete ten thousand worlds with halfe a Span:
Whose Might Almighty can by half a looks
Root up the rocks and rock the hills by th' roots.
Can take this mighty World up in his hande,
And shake it like a Squitchen[2] or a Wand.
Whose single Frown will make the Heavens shake
Like as an aspen leafe the Winde makes quake.
Oh! what a might is this! Whose single frown
Doth shake the world as it would shake it down?
Which All from Nothing fet, from Nothing, All:
Hath All on Nothing set, lets Nothing fall.

Gave All to nothing Man indeed, whereby
Through nothing man all might him Glorify.
In Nothing is imbosst the brightest Gem
More pretious than all pretiousness in them.
But Nothing man did throw down all by sin:
And darkened that lightsom Gem in him,
   That now his Brightest Diamond is grown
   Darker by far than any Coalpit Stone.

Prologue

Lord, Can a Crumb of Earth the Earth outweigh:[1]
    Outmatch all mountains, nay the Chrystall Sky?
Imbosom in't designs that shall Display
    And trace into the Boundless Deity?
    Yea, hand a Pen whose moysture doth guild ore
    Eternall Glory with a glorious glore.[2]

If it its Pen had of an Angels Quill,
    And sharpend on a Pretious Stone ground tite,
And dipt in Liquid Gold, and mov'de by skill
    In Christall leaves should golden Letters write,
    It would but blot and blur: yea, jag and jar,
    Unless thou mak'st the Pen and Scribener.

I am this Crumb of Dust which is design'd
    To make my Pen unto thy Praise alone,
And my dull Phancy I would gladly grinde
    Unto an Edge on Zions Pretious Stone:
    And Write in Liquid Gold upon thy Name
    My Letters till thy glory forth doth flame.

Let not th' attempts breake down my Dust I pray,
    Nor laugh thou them to scorn, but pardon give.
Inspire this Crumb of Dust till it display
    Thy Glory through 't: and then thy dust shall live.
    Its failings then thou'lt overlook I trust,
    They being Slips slipt from thy Crumb of Dust.

Thy Crumb of Dust breaths two words from its breast;
    That thou wilt guide its pen to write aright
To Prove thou art, and that thou art the best,
    And shew thy Properties[3] to shine most bright.
    And then thy Works will shine as flowers on Stems,
    Or as in Jewellary Shops, do jems.

The Effects of Mans Apostacy

While man unmarr'd abode, his Spirits all
In Vivid hue were active in their hall,
This Spotless Body; here and there mentain
Their traffick for the Universall gain,
Till Sin Beat up for Volunteers. Whence came
A thousand Griefs attending on the same.
Which march in ranck and file, proceed to make
A Battery, and the fort of Life to take.
Which when the Centinalls did spy, the Heart
Did beate alarum up in every part.
The Vitall Spirits apprehend thereby
Exposde to danger great the suburbs ly,
The which they do desert, and speedily
The Fort of Life the Heart, they Fortify.
The Heart beats up still by her Pulse to Call
Out of the outworks her train Souldiers all
Which quickly come hence: now the Looks grow pale,
Limbs feeble too: the Enemies prevaile:
Do scale the Outworks where there's Scarce a Scoute
That can be Spi'de sent from the Castle out.

Man at a muze, and in a maze doth stand,
While Feare, the Generall of all the Band,
Makes inroads on him: then he Searches why,
And quickly findes, God stand as Enemy,
Whom he would fain subdue, yet Fears affright
In Varnishing their Weapons in his sight.
Troops after troops, Bands after Bands do high,
Armies of armed terrours drawing nigh:
He lookes within, and sad amazement's there,
Without, and all things fly about his Eares,
Above, and sees Heaven falling on his pate,
Below, and spies th' Infernall burning lake,
Before, and sees God storming in his Face;
Behinde, and spies Vengeance persues his trace:
To stay he dares not, go he knows not where:

From God he can't, to God he dreads for Feare.
To Dy he Dreads; For Vengeance's due to him;
To Live he must not, Death persues his Sin:
He Knows not what to have, nor what to loose,
Nor what to do, nor what to take or Choose;
Thus over Stretcht upon the Wrack of Woe,
Bereav'd of Reason, he proceeds now so.
Betakes himselfe unto his Heels in hast,
Runs like a Madman till his Spirits wast,
Then like a Child that fears the Poker Clapp
Him on his face doth on his Mothers lap
Doth hold his breath, lies still for fear least hee
Should by his breathing lowd discover'd bee.
Thus on his face doth see no outward thing,
But still his heart for Feare doth pant within;
Doth make its Drummer beate so loud it makes
The Very Bulworks of the City Quake:
Yet gets no aide: Wherefore the Spirits they
Are ready all to leave, and run away.
For Nature in this Pannick feare scarce gives
Him life enough, to let him feel he lives.
Yet this he easily feels, he liveth in
A Dying Life, and Living Death by Sin.
Yet in this Lifeless life wherein he lies,
Some Figments of Excuses doth devise
That he may Something say, when rain'd, although
His Say seems nothing, and for nought will go.
But while he Sculking on his face close lies,
Espying nought, the Eye Divine him spies.
Justice and Mercy then fall to debate
Concerning this poore fallen mans estate.
Before the Bench of the Almighties Breast
Th' ensuing Dialogues hint their Contest.

A Dialogue between Justice and Mercy

Offended Justice comes in fiery Rage,
   Like to a Rampant Lyon new assaild,
Array'de in Flaming fire now to engage,
   With red hot burning Wrath, poore man unbaild,
   In whose Dread Vissage sinfull man may spy
   Confounding, Rending, Flaming Majesty.

Out Rebell, out (saith Justice), to the Wrack,
   Which every joynt unjoynts, doth streatch and strain,
Where Sinews tortur'de are untill they Crack,
   And Flesh is torn asunder grain by grain.
   What! Spit thy Venom in my Face? Come out
   To handy gripes, seing thou art so stoute.

Mercy takes up the Challenge, Comes as meeke
   As any Lamb, on mans behalfe she speakes;
Like new blown pincks, breaths out perfumed reech,[1]
   And doth revive the heart before it breaks.
   Justice (saith Mercy) if thou Storm so fast,
   Man is but dust that flies before thy blast.

JUSTICE

My Essence is ingag'de, I cannot bate,
   Justice not done no Justice is; and hence
I cannot hold off of the Rebells pate
   The Vengeance he halls down with Violence.
   If Justice wronged be, she must revenge:
   Unless a way be found to make all friends.

MERCY

My Essence is engag'de pitty to show:
   Mercy not done no Mercy is, and hence
I'le put my shoulders to the burden, so
   Halld on his head with hands of Violence.
   As Justice justice evermore must doe:
   So Mercy mercy evermore must show.

JUSTICE

I'le take thy Bond: But know thou this must doe:
   Thou from thy Fathers bosom must depart,
And be incarnate like a slave below,
    Must pay mans Debts unto [the] utmost marke.
    Thou must sustain that burden, that will make
    The Angells sink into th' Infernall lake.

Nay, on thy shoulders bare must beare the Smart
   Which makes the Stoutest Angell buckling cry;
Nay, makes thy Soule to Cry through griefe of heart,
    ELI, ELI, LAMA SABACHT[H]ANI,
    If this thou wilt, come then, and do not spare:
    Beare up the Burden on thy shoulders bare.

MERCY

All this I'le do, and do it o're and o're,
   Before my Clients Case shall ever faile.
I'le pay his Debt, and wipe out all his Score,
    And till the pay day Come, I'le be his baile.
    I Heaven and Earth do on my shoulders beare,
    Yet down I'le throw them all rather than Spare.

JUSTICE

Yet notwithstanding still this is too Small,
   Although there was a thousand times more done,
If sinless man did, sinfull man will fall:
    If out of debt, will on a new score run.
    Then stand away, and let me strike at first:
    For better now, than when he's at the Worst.

MERCY

If more a thousand times too little bee,
   Ten thousand times yet more than this I'le do:
I'le free him from his Sin, and Set him free
    From all those faults the which he's subject to.
    Then Stand away, and strike not at the first:
    He'l better grow when he is at the worst.

JUSTICE

Nay, this ten thousand times as much can still
    Confer no hony to the Sinners hive.
For man though shrived throughly from all ill,
    His Righteousness is merely negative.
        Though none be damnd but such as sin imbrace:
        Yet none are sav'd without Inherent Grace.

MERCY

What though ten thousand times, too little bee?
    I will-ten thousand thousand times more do.
I will not onely from his Sin him free,
    But fill him with Inherent grace also.
        Though none are Sav'd that wickedness imbrace,
        Yet none are Damn'd that have Inherent Grace.

JUSTICE

Yet this ten thousand thousand times more shall,
    Though Doubled o're and o're, for little stands;
The Righteousness of God should be his all,
    The which he cannot have for want of hands.
        Then though he's spar'de at first, at last he'l fall
        For want of hands to hold himselfe withall.

MERCY

Though this ten thousand thousand times much more,
    Though doubled o're and o're for little go,
I'le double still its double o're and o're,
    And trible that untill I make it do.
        I'le make him hands of Faith to hold full fast:
        Spare him at first, then he'l not fall at last.

For by these hands he'l lay his Sins upon
    The Scape Goats head, o're whom he shall Confess,
And with these hands he rightly shall put on
    My milkwhite Robe of Lovely Righteousness.
        Now Justice, on! thy Will fulfilled bee:
        Thou dost no wrong: the Sinner's just like thee.

JUSTICE

If so, it's so, then I'le his Quittance seale:
   Or shall accuse myselfe as well as him:
If so, I, Justice, shall of Justice faile,
   Which if I do, Justice herselfe should sin.
   Justice unspotted is; and therefore must
[   ]¹

MERCY

I do foresee Proud man will me abuse,
   He'th broke his Legs, yet's Legs his stilts must bee:
And I may stand untill the Chilly Dews
   Do pearle my Locks before he'l stand on mee.
   For set a Beggar upon horseback, see,
   He'll ride as if no man so good as hee.²

JUSTICE

And I foresee Proude man will me abuse,
   Judging his Shekel is the Sanctuaries:
He on his durty stilts to walk will Choose:
   Yea, is as Clean as I, and nothing Varies:
   Although his Shekel is not Silver good,
   And's tilting stilts do stick within the mudd.

MERCY

But most he'l me abuse, I feare, for still
   Some will have Farms to farm, some wives to wed:
Some beasts to buy; and I must waite their Will.
   Though while they scrape their naile or scratch their head,
   Nay, though with Cap in hand I Wooe them long,
   They'l whistle out their Whistle e're they'l come.

JUSTICE

I see I'st be abus'de by greate and small:
   And most will count me blinde, or will not see:
Me leaden heel'd, with iron hands they'l Call:
   Or am unjust, or they more just than mee.
   And while they while away their Mercy so,
   They set their bristles up at Justice do.

MERCY

I feare the Humble Soul will be too shie;
  Judging my Mercy lesser than his Sin.
Inlarging this, but lessening that thereby.
  'S if Mercy would not Mercy be to him.
  Alas! poore Heart! how art thou damnifi'de
  By Proud Humility and Humble Pride?

JUSTICE

The Humble Soul deales worse with me, doth Cry,
  If I be just, I'le on him Vengeance take:
As if I su'de Debtor and Surety,
  And double Debt and intrest too would rake.
  If Justice sue the Bonds that Cancelld are,
  Sue Justice then before a juster bar.

MERCY

But in this Case, alas, what must be done
  That haughty souls may humble be, and low?
That Humble souls may suck the Hony Comb?
  And thou for Justice, I for Mercy, go?
  This Query weighty is, Let's therefore shew
  What must be done herein by me and you.

JUSTICE

Lest that the Soule in Sin securely ly,
  And do neglect Free Grace, I'le step[p]ing in,
Convince him by the Morall Law, whereby
  Ile'st se[e] in what a pickle he is in.
  For all he hath, for nothing stand it shall,
  If of the Law one hair breadth short it fall.

MERCY

And lest the Soule should quite discourag'de stand,
  I will step in, and smile him in the face,
Nay, I to him will hold out in my hand
  The golden scepter of my Rich-Rich Grace:
  Intreating him with smiling lips most cleare,
  At Court of Justice in my robes t' appeare.

JUSTICE

If any after Satans Pipes do Caper,
   Red burning Coales from hell in Wrath I gripe,
And make them in his face with Vengeance Vaper,
   Untill he dance after the Gospell Pipe.
    Whose Sun is Sin, when Sin in Sorrow's shrow'd,
    Their Sun of Joy sets in a grievous Cloud.

MERCY

When any such are startled from ill,
   And cry help, help, with tears, I will advance
The Musick of the Gospell Minsterill,
   Whose strokes they strike, and tunes exactly dance.
    Who mourn when Justice frowns, when Mercie playes
    Will to her sounding Viall Chant out Praise.

JUSTICE

The Works of Merit-Mongers I will weigh
   Within the Ballance of the sanctuary:
Their Matter and their Manner I will lay
   Unto the Standard-Rule t'see how they vary.
    Whos'ever trust doth, to his golden deed
    Doth rob a barren Garden for a Weed.

MERCY

Yet if they'l onely on my Merits trust,
   They'st in Gods Paradise themselves solace;
Their beauteous garden knot I'le also thrust
   With Royall Slips, Sweet Flowers, and Herbs of Grace.
    Their Knots I'le weed, to give a spangling show
    In Order: and perfumes shall from them flow.

JUSTICE

Those that are ignorant, and do not know
   What meaneth Sin, nor what means Sanctity,
I will Convince that all save Saints must go
   Into hot fire, and brimston there to fry:
    Whose Pains hot scalding boyling Lead transcends,
    But evermore adds more, and never Ends.

MERCY

Though simple, learn of mee; I will you teach
   True Wisdom for your Souls Felicity;
Wisdom Extending to the Endless reach
    And blissfull end of all Eternity;
     Wisdom that doth all else transcend as far
     As Sol's bright Glory doth a painted Star.

JUSTICE

You that Extenuate your sins, come see
   Them in Gods multiplying Glass: for here
Your little sins will just like mountains bee;
    And as they are, just so they will appeare.
     Who doth a little sin Extenuate
     Extends the same, and two thereof doth make.

MERCY

A little sin is sin: and is Sin Small?
   Excuse it not, but aggrivate it more,
Lest that your little Sin asunder fall
    And two become, each bigger than before.
     Who scants his sin will scarce get grace to save,
     For little Sins but little pardons have.

JUSTICE

Unto the Humble Humble Soule I say,
   Cheer up, poor Heart, for satisfi'de am I.
For Justice nothing to thy Charge can lay;
    Thou hast Acquittance in thy surety.
     The Court of Justice thee acquits: therefore
     Thou to the Court of Mercy are bound o're.

MERCY

My Dove, come hither, linger not, nor stay.
   Though thou among the pots hast lain, behold
Thy wings with Silver Colours I'le o'relay:
    And lay thy feathers o're with yellow gold.
     Justice in Justice must adjudge thee just:
     If thou in Mercies Mercy put thy trust.

Mans Perplexity When Call'd to an Account

Justice and Mercy ending their Contest,
In such a sort, now thrust away the Desk.
And other titles come in Majesty,
All to attend Almighty royally:
Which sparkle out, call man to come and tell
How he his Cloath defil'd, and how he fell.

He on his skirts with Guilt and Filth out peeps,
With Pallid Pannick Fear upon his Cheeks,
With Trembling joynts, and Quivering Lips, doth quake,
As if each word he was about to make
Should hackt asunder be, and Chopt as small
As Potherbs for the pot, before they Call
Upon the Understanding to draw neer,
By tabbering on the Drum within the eare.
His Spirits are so low they'l scarce afford
Him Winde enough to wast a single word
Over the Tongue unto one's eare: yet loe,
This tale at last with sobs and sighs lets goe:
Saying, 'my Mate procur'de me all this hurt,
Who threw me in my best Cloaths in the Dirt.'

Thus man hath lost his Freehold by his ill:
Now to his Land Lord tenent is at Will,
And must the Tenement keep in repare,
Whate're the ruins and the Charges are.
Nay, and must mannage war against his Foes;
Although ten thousand strong, he must oppose.
Some seeming Friends prove secret foes, which will
Thrust Fire i' th' thatch; nay, Stob,[1] Cut throate, and kill.
Some undermine the Walls. Some knock them down,
And make them tumble on the Tenents Crown.
  He's then turnd out of Doors, and so must stay,
  Till's house be rais'd against the Reckoning day.

43

Gods Selecting Love in the Decree

Man in this Lapst Estate at very best,
A Cripple is, and footsore, sore opprest.
Can't track Gods Trace, but Pains and pritches prick
Like poyson'd splinters sticking in the Quick.
Yet jims[1] in th' Downy path with pleasures spread,
As 'twas below him on the Earth to tread;
Can prance and trip within the way of Sin,
Yet in Gods path moves not a little wing.

Almighty this foreseing, and withall
That all this stately worke of his would fall,
Tumble, and Dash to pieces, Did inlay,
Before it was too late for it, a Stay;
Doth with his hands hold and uphold the same:
Hence his Eternall Purpose doth proclaim,
Whereby transcendently he makes to shine
Transplendent Glory in his Grace Divine.
Almighty makes a mighty sumptuous feast:
Doth make the Sinfull Sons of men his guests.
But yet in speciall Grace he hath to some,
(Because they Cripples are, and Cannot come)
He sends a Royall Coach forth for the same,
To fetch them in, and names them name by name.
A Royall Coach whose scarlet Canopy
O're silver Pillars, doth expanded ly:
All bottomed with purest gold refin'de,
And inside, o're with lovely Love all lin'de.
Which Coach indeed you may exactly spy
All mankinde splits in a Dic[h]otomy.[2]
  For all ride to the feast that favour finde,
  The rest do slite the Call, and stay behinde.

O! Honour! Honour! Honour! Oh! the Gain!
And all such Honours all the saints obtain.
It is the Chariot of the King of Kings:
That all who Glory gain, to glory brings;

Whose Glory makes the rest, (when spi'de) beg in.
Some gaze and stare, some stranging at the thing,
Some peep therein; some rage thereat, but all,
Like market people seing on a stall
Some rare Commodity, Clap hands thereon,
And Cheapen 't hastily, but soon are gone
For hearing of the price, and wanting pay,
Do pish thereat, and Coily pass away.
So hearing of the terms, whist! they'le abide
At home before they'l pay so much to ride.
But they to whom it's sent had rather all
Dy in this Coach, than let their journey fall.
They up therefore do get, and in it ride
Unto Eternal bliss, while down the tide
The other scull unto eternall woe,
By letting slip their former journey so.
For when they finde the Silver Pillars fair,
The Golden bottom pav'de with Love as rare,
To be the Spirits sumptuous building cleare;
When in the Soul his Temple he doth reare,
And Purple Canopy to bee (they spy)
All Graces Needlework and Huswifry;
Their stomachs rise: these graces will not down:
They think them Slobber Sawces:[1] therefore frown.
They loath the same, wamble keck,[2] heave they do:
Their Spleen thereat out at their mouths they throw.
Which while they do, the Coach away doth high:
Wheeling the Saints in't to eternall joy.
 These therefore and their journey now do come
 For to be treated on, and Coacht along.

The Frowardness of the Elect in the Work of Conversion

Those upon whom Almighty doth intend
His all Eternall Glory to expend,
Lulld in the lap of sinfull Nature snugg,
Like Pearls in Puddles cover'd ore with mudd:
Whom, if you search, perhaps some few you'l finde,
That to notorious Sins were ne're inclinde:
Some shunning some, some most, some greate, some small;
Some this, that, or the other, some none at all.
But all, or almost all, you'st easly finde,
To all, or almost all Defects inclinde:
To Revell with the Rabble rout who say,
'Let's hiss this Piety out of our Day.'
And those whose frame is made of finer twine
Stand further off from Grace than Wash from Wine.
Those who suck Grace from th' breast,[1] are nigh as rare
As Black Swans that in milkwhite Rivers are.
Grace therefore calls them all, and sweetly wooes.
Some won come in, the rest as yet refuse,
And run away: Mercy persues apace,
Then some Cast down their arms, Cry Quarter, Grace!
Some Chased out of breath, drop down with feare,
Perceiving the persuer drawing neer.
The rest persude, divide into two rancks,
And this way one, and that the other prancks.

Then in comes Justice with her forces by her,
And doth persue as hot as sparkling fire.
The right wing then begins to fly away:
But in the streights strong Baracadoes lay.
They're therefore forc'd to face about, and have
Their spirits Quel'd, and therefore Quarter Crave.
These Captivde thus, Justice persues the Game
With all her troops to take the other train.
Which being Chast in a Peninsula
And followd close, they finde no other way

To make escape, but t' rally round about:
Which if it faile them that they get not out,
They're forct into the Infernall Gulfe alive,
Or hackt in pieces are, or took Captive
But spying Mercy stand with Justice, they
Cast down their Weapons, and for Quarter pray.
Their lives are therefore spar'de, yet they are ta'ne
As th'other band: and prisoners must remain.
And so they must now Justice's Captives bee
On Mercies Quarrell: Mercy sets not free.
    Their former Captain is their Deadly foe,
    And now, poor souls, they know not what to do.

Satans Rage at them in their Conversion

Grace by the Aid of Justice wins the day,
And Satans Captives, Captives leads away:
Who finding of their former Captains Cheates,
To be Rebellion, him a Rebell Greate,
Against his Rightfull Sovereign, by whom
He shortly shall to Execution Come:
They sue[1] for Pardon do at Mercies Doore,
Bewailing of that war they wag'd before.

Then Satan in a red-hot firy rage
Comes bell[ow]ing, roaring, ready to ingage,
To rend and tare in pieces small, all those
Whom in the former Quarrell he did lose.
But's boyling Poyson'd madness, being by
A Shield Divine repelld, he thus lets fly:
'You Rebells all, I Will you gripe and fist;
I'le make my Jaws a Mill to grin'de such grists.
Look not for Mercy; Mercy well doth see
You'l be more false to her than Unto mee.
You're the first Van that fell; you're Traitors, Foes;
And Unto such, Grace will no trust repose.
You Second Ranck are Cowards; if Christ Come
With you to fight his field, you'l from him run.
You third are feeble-hearted; if Christs Crown
Must stand or fall by you, you'l fling it down.
You last did last the longest: but being ta'ne,
Are Prisoners made, and Jayle Birds must remain.
It had been better on the Turff to dy,
Then in such Deadly slavery to ly.
Nay, at the best you all are Captive Foes.
Will Wisdom have no better aid than those?
Trust to a forced Faith? To hearts well known
To be (like yours) to all black Treason Prone?
For when I shall let fly at you, you'l fall:
And so fall foule Upon your Generall.
Hee'l Hang you up alive then, by and by;

And I'le you wrack too for your treachery.
He will become your foe; you then shall bee
Flanckt of by him before, behinde by mee.
You'st stand between us two our spears to dunce.[1]
Can you Offend and Fence both wayes at once?
You'l then have sharper service than the Whale,
Between the swordfish, and the Threshers taile.
You'l then be mawld worse than the hand that's right
Between the heads of Wheelhorn'd Rams that fight.
    What will you do when you shall squezed bee
    Between such Monstrous Gyants Jaws as Wee?'

The Souls Address to Christ against these Assaults

Thou Gracious Lord, Our Honour'd Generall,
  May't suite thy Pleasure never to impute
It our Presumption, when presume we shall,
  To line thy Noble Ears with our Greate suite?
  With ropes about our necks we come, and lie
  Before thy pleasure's Will and Clemency.

When we unto the height of Sin were grown,
  We sought thy Throne to overthrow; but were
In this our seeking Quickly overthrown:
  A Mass of Mercy in thy face shone cleare.
  We quarter had: though if we'de had our share,
  We had been quarter'd up as Rebells are.

Didst thou thy Grace on Treators arch expend?
  And force thy Favour on thy stubborn Foe?
And hast no Favour for a failing Friend,
  That in thy Quarrell trippeth with his toe?
  If thus it be, thy Foes Speed better far,
  Than do thy Friends, that go to fight thy War.

But is it as the Adversary said?
  Dost thou not hear his murdering Canons roare?
What Vollies fly? What Ambushments are laid?
  And still his stratagems grow more and more.
  Lord, fright this frightfull Enemy away.
  A Trip makes not a Traitor: Spare, we pray.

And if thou still suspect us, come and search:
  Pluck out our hearts and search them narrowly.
If Sin allow'd in any Corner learch,
  We beg a Pardon and a Remedy.
  Lord, Gybbit up such Rebells Arch, Who do
  Set ope the back doore to thy Cursed foe.

Christs Reply

I am a Captain to your Will;
   You found me Gracious, so shall still,
Whilst that my Will is your Design.
   If that you stick unto my Cause,
   Opposing whom oppose my Laws,
I am your own, and you are mine.

   The weary Soule I will refresh,
   And Ease him of his heaviness.
Who'le slay a Friend? And save a Foe?
   Who in my War do take delight,
   Fight not for prey, but Pray and Fight,
Although they slip, I'le mercy show.

   Then Credit not your Enemy,
   Whose Chiefest daintie is a lie:
I will you comfort sweet extend.
   Behold I am a sun and shield,
   And a sharp sword to win the field:
I'l surely Crown you in the End.

   His murdering Canons which do roare,
   And Engins[1] though as many more,
Shoot onely aire: no Bullets fly.
   Unless you dare him with your Crest,
   And ope to him the naked breast,
Small Execution's done thereby.

To him that smiteth hip and thigh
   My foes as his: Walks warily,
I'le give him Grace: he'st give me praise.
   Let him whose foot doth hit a stone
   Through weakness, not rebellion,
Not faint, but think on former dayes.

The Effect of this Reply with a fresh Assault
from Satan

Like as the Shining Sun, we do behold,
Is hot and Light, when th' Weather waxeth Cold:
Like as brave Valour in a Captain, steels
His Armies Courage, when their spirit reels:
As Aqua Vitae[1] when the Vitalls faile:
So doth this speech the Drooping Soul availe.
How doth this Answer Mercies Captives Cheer!
Yet those whom Justice took still Drooping were.
And in this nick of time the Foe, through spite,
Doth like a glorious Angell seem of Light.
Yet though he painteth o're his Velvet smut,
He Cannot yet Conceal his Cloven foot.
Hence in their joy, he straweth poyson on
Those Objects that their senses feed upon.
By some odde straggling thought, up poyson flies
Into the heart, and through the Eares and Eyes:
Which sick, lies gasping. Other thoughts then high
To hold its head, and Venom'd are thereby.
Hence they are influenc't to selfe Ends: these darts
Strike secret swelling Pride up in their hearts.
 The which he fosters till the bladder flies
 In pieces, then joy lies agast and dies.

Now Satan counts the Cast his own thus thrown:
Off goes the Angels Coate, on goes his own;
With Griping Paws, and Goggling Eyes draws nigher,
Like some fierce Shagg'd Red Lion, belching fire:
Doth stoutly Charge them home that they did fall
And breake the Laws of their Choice Admirall,
And his attend: and so were his. For they
Must needs be his whom ever they obey.
Thus he in frightfull wise assaults them all;
Then one by one doth singly on them fall:
 Doth winnow them with all his wiles, he can,
 As Wheate is winnow'd with the Sieve and Fan.

First Satans Assault against those that first Came up to Mercys terms

SATAN

Soon ripe, soon rot. Young Saint, Old Divell. Loe!
Why to an Empty Whistle did you goe?
What! Come Uncalld? And Run Unsent for? Stay
It's Childrens Bread. Hands off: out, Dogs, away.

SOUL

It's not an Empty Whistle: yet withall,
And if it be a Whistle, then a Call:
A Call to Childrens Bread, which take we may.
Thou onely art the Dog whipt hence away.

SATAN

If I, then you: for by Apostasy
You are the Imps of Death as much [as] I.
And Death doth reign o're you through Sin; you see,
As well as Sin doth reign to Death in mee.

SOUL

It is deni'd: Gods Mercy taking place,
Prepared Grace for us, and us for Grace.
And Graces Coach in Grace hath fetcht us in
Unto her Feast. We shall not dy in Sin.

SATAN

If it be so, your sins are Crucifide:
Which if they be, they struggl'd when they di'de.
It is not so with you: you judge before
You felt them gird, you'de got them out of Doore.

SOUL

Mercy the Quartermaster speedily
Did stifle Sin, and still its hidious Cry:
Whose Knife at first stuck in its heart to th' head:
That sin, before it hard did sprunt,[1] fell dead.

53

SATAN

A mere Delusion! Nature shows that Life
Will strugle most upon the bloody Knife.
And so will Sin. Nay, Christ doth onely Call,
And offer ease to such as are in thrall.

SOUL

He offer'd unto mee, and I receiv'd.
Of what hee wrought, I am not yet bereav'd.
Though Justice set Amercement[1] on mee,
Mercy hath took it off, and set me free.

SATAN

Is Mercy impudent? or Justice blind?
I am to make distraint on thee Design'd.
The North must wake before the South proves Kind:[2]
The Law must breake before the Gospell binde.

SOUL

But Giliads Balm,[3] like Balsom heald my wound;
Makes not the Patient sore, yet leaves him sound.
The Gospell did the Law prevent: my heart
Is therefore dresst from Sin: and did not smart.

SATAN

A likely thing! Oh shame! presume on Grace!
Here's Sin in Grain: it hath a Double Face.
Come, Come with mee. I'le shew your Outs and Inns,
Your Inside and your out: your Holy things.
    For these I will anatomize; then see:
    Believe your very Eyes, believe not mee.

The Accusation of the Inward Man

You want Cleare Spectacles: your eyes are dim:
Turn inside out, and turn your Eyes within.
Your sins like motes in th' sun do swim: nay, see
Your Mites are Molehills, Molehills Mountains bee.
Your Mountain Sins do magnitude transcend:
Whose number's numberless, and doth want end.
The Understanding's dark, and therefore Will
Account of Ill for Good, and Good for ill.
As to a Purblinde man men oft appeare
Like Walking Trees within the Hemisphere,
So in the judgment Carnall things Excell:
Pleasures and Profits beare away the Bell.
The Will is hereupon perverted so,
It laquyes after ill; doth good foregoe.
The Reasonable Soule doth much delight
A Pickpack t' ride o' th' Sensuall Appetite.
And hence the heart is hardened, and toyes
With Love, Delight, and Joy, yea Vanities.

Make but a thorow search, and you may spy
Your soul a trudging hard, though secretly
Upon the feet of your Affections mute,
And hankering after all forbidden fruite.
Ask but yourselfe in secret, laying neer
Thy head thereto: 'twill Whisper in thine eare
That it is tickled much, though secretly.
And greatly itches after Vilany.
'Twill fleere[1] thee in thy face, and though it say
It must not tell, it scorns to tell thee nay.
But Slack the rains, and Come a Loophole lower:
You'l finde it was but Pen-coop't up before.
Nay, muster up your thoughts, and take the Pole
Of what walk in the Entry of your Soule:
Which if you do, you certainly will finde
With Robbers, Cut-throats, Theives it's mostly lin'de.
And hundred Roagues you'l finde ly gaming there:

For one true man, that in that path appears.
Your True man too's oft footsore, sildom is
Sound Winde and Limb: and still to add to this,
He's but a Traviller within that Way:
Whereas the rest there pitch their Tents, and stay.
Nay, nay, what thoughts Unclean? Lascivious?
Blasphemous? Murderous? and Malicious?
Tyranick? Wrathfull? Atheistick rise
Of Evils New and Old, of e'ry Sise?
These bed and board here; make the heart a sty
Of all Abominable Brothlery.

    Then is it pure? is this the fruite of Grace?
    If so, how do yee: You and I Embrace!

The Outward Man accused

Turn o're thy Outward man, and judge aright.
Doth not a Pagans Life out Shine thy Light?
Thy fleering Looks, thy Wanton Eyes, each part
Are Painted Sign-Post of a Wanton heart.
If thou art weigh'd in Golden Scales, Dost do
To others as thou wouldst be done unto?
Weigh, weigh thy Words: thy Untruths, all which came
Out of thy mouth, and thou Confest the same.
Why did thy Tongue detract from any one,
Whisper such tales thou wouldst not have be known?
When thou was got in such a merry veane,
How far didst thou exceed the golden mean?
When that thou wast at such a Boon or Feast,
Why didst thou rather ly than lose thy jeast?
How wast thou tickled when thy droughty Eares
Allay'de their Thirst with filthy squibs and jears?
Why didst thou glaver¹ men of place? And why
Scowle, Glout, and Frown on honest Poverty?
Why did'st thou spend thy State in foolish prancks?
And Peacock up thyselfe above thy rancks?
Why thoughtst thyselfe out of the World as shut,
When not with others in the Cony Cut?²
Hold up thy head; is't thus or no? if yea,
How then is all thy folly purgd away?
   If no, thy tongue belies itselfe, for loe
   Thou saidst thy heart was dresst from sin also.

The Soul accused in its Serving God

When thou dost go to serve thy God, behold
What greate Distractions do thy Soule infold?
How thy Religious Worship's much abusde?
And with Confusion greate thy Soul's amus'de?
What thoughts to God on Errand dost thou send
That have not Sin therein, or in the end?
In Holy-Waters I delight to fish,
For then I mudd them, or attain a Dish
Of Holy things. I oft have Chiefest part
And Cutting: nay, do Carve the fat and heart.
For in Gods worship still thy heart doth cling
Unto and follows toyish Earthly things.
And what thou offer'st God, his Holy Eye
Sees is an Offering of Hypocrisy.
And if thou saw'st no hell nor heaven, I see
My Soule for thine, thy Soule and mine agree.
What then's thy Love to God, and Piety?
Is it not selfish? And comes in by th' by?
For selfe is all thine aim; not God thine end:
And what Delight hath he in such a friend?
Lip Love is little else, but such a ly
As makes the matter but Hypocrisy.

What's thy Repentance? Can'st thou come and show
By those salt Rivers which do Ebb and Flow,
By th' motion of that Ocean Vast within,
Of pickled sorrow rising for thy sin?
For sin prooves very Costly unto all:
It Cost Saint Peter bitter tears, and Paul.
Thy joy is groundless, Faith is false; thy Hope
Presumption, and Desire is almost broke.
Zeale Wildfire is; thy Pray'res are sapless most,
Or like the Whistling of some Dead mans Ghost.
Thy Holy Conference is onely like
An Empty Voice that tooteth through a pipe;
Thy Soule doth peep out at thine Eares and Eyes

To bless those bawbles that are earthly toyes.
But when Gods Words in at those Windows peepe
To kiss thy Soul, thy Soul lies dead asleep.
Examine but thy Conscience: her reply
Will suite hereto: For Conscience dare not ly.
When did thine Eyes run down for sin as sin,
That thus thy heart runs up with joy to sing?
    Thy sins do sculk under a flowrisht paint;
    Hence thou a Sinner art, or I a Saint.

SOUL

Well, Satan, well: with thee I'le parle no more.
But do adjure thee hence: begone therefore.
If I as yet was thine, I thus do say
I from thy flag would quickly flag away.
    Begone therefore; to him I'le send a groane
    Against thee drawn, who makes my heart his Throne.

The Souls Groan to Christ for Succour

Good Lord, behold this Dreadfull Enemy
   Who makes me tremble with his fierce assaults;
I dare not trust, yet feare to give the ly,
   For in my soul, my soul finds many faults.
   And though I justify myselfe to's face:
   I do Condemn myselfe before thy Grace.

He strives to mount my sins, and them advance
   Above thy Merits, Pardons, or Good Will;
Thy Grace to lessen, and thy Wrath t' inhance
   As if thou couldst not pay the sinners bill.
   He Chiefly injures thy rich Grace, I finde,
   Though I confess my heart to sin inclin'de.

Those Graces which thy Grace enwrought in mee,
   He makes as nothing but a pack of Sins;
He maketh Grace no grace, but Crueltie;
   Is Graces Honey Comb, a Comb of Stings?
   This makes me ready leave thy Grace and run,
   Which if I do, I finde I am undone.

I know he is thy Cur, therefore I bee
   Perplexed lest I from thy Pasture stray,
He bayghs and barks so veh'mently at mee.
   Come, rate this Cur, Lord, breake his teeth I pray.
   Remember me I humbly pray thee first,
   Then halter up this Cur that is so Curst.

Christs Reply

Peace, Peace, my Hony, do not Cry,
My Little Darling, wipe thine eye,
   Oh Cheer, Cheer up, come see.
Is anything too deare, my Dove,
Is anything too good, my Love,
   To get or give for thee?

If in the severall thou art,
This Yelper fierce will at thee bark:
   That thou art mine this shows.
As Spot barks back the sheep again,
Before they to the Pound are ta'ne,
   So he, and hence 'way goes.

But if this Cur that bayghs so sore,
Is broken tootht, and muzzled sure,
   Fear not, my Pritty Heart.
His barking is to make thee Cling
Close underneath thy Saviours wing.
   Why did my sweeten start?

And if he run an inch too fur,
I'le Check his Chain, and rate the Cur.
   My Chick, keep close to mee.
The Poles shall sooner kiss and greet,
And Paralells shall sooner meet,
   Than thou shall harmed bee.

He seeks to aggrivate thy sin,
And screw them to the highest pin,
   To make thy faith to quaile.
Yet mountain sins like mites should show,
And then these mites for naught should goe,
   Could he but once prevaile.

I smote thy sins upon the Head.
They Dead'ned are, though not quite dead:

And shall not rise again.
I'l put away the Guilt thereof,
And purge its Filthiness cleare off:
   My Blood doth out the stain.

And though thy judgment was remiss,
Thy Headstrong Will too Wilfull is:
   I will Renew the same.
And though thou do too frequently
Offend as heretofore, hereby
   I'le not severely blaim.

And though thy senses do inveagle
Thy Noble Soul to tend the Beagle,
   That t' hunt her games forthgo.
I'le Lure her back to me, and Change
Those fond Affections that do range
   As yelping beagles doe.

Although thy sins increase their race,
And though when thou hast sought for Grace,
   Thou fallst more than before:
If thou by true Repentence Rise,
And Faith makes me thy Sacrifice,
   I'l pardon all, though more.

Though Satan strive to block thy way
By all his Stratagems he may,
   Come, come, though through the fire.
For Hell, that Gulph of fire for sins,
Is not so hot as t' burn thy Shins.
   Then Credit not the Lyar.

Those Cursed Vermin Sins that Crawle
All ore thy Soul, both Greate and Small,
   Are onely Satans own:
Which he in his Malignity
Unto thy Souls true Sanctity
   In at the doore hath thrown.

And though they be Rebellion high,
Ath'ism or Apostacy:
   Though blasphemy it bee:
Unto what Quality, or Sise,
Excepting one, so e're it rise,
   Repent, I'le pardon thee.

Although thy Soule was once a Stall
Rich hung with Satans nicknacks all;
   If thou Repent thy Sin,
A Tabernacle in 't I'le place,
Fil[l']d with God[s] Spirit, and his Grace.
   Oh Comfortable thing!

I dare the World therefore to show
A God like me, to anger slow:
   Whose wrath is full of Grace.
Doth hate all Sins both Greate and Small:
Yet when Repented, pardons all.
   Frowns with a Smiling Face.

As for thy outward Postures each,
Thy Gestures, Actions, and thy Speech,
   I Eye, and Eying spare,
If thou repent. My Grace is more
Ten thousand times still tribled ore
   Than thou canst want, or ware.

As for the Wicked Charge he makes,
That he of Every Dish first takes
   Of all thy holy things:
It's false; deny the same, and say,
That which he had he stool away
   Out of thy Offerings.

Though to thy Griefe, poor Heart, thou finde
In Pray're too oft a wandring minde,
   In Sermons, Spirits dull:
Though faith in firy furnace flags,

63

And Zeale in Chilly Seasons lags:
  Temptations powerfull:

These faults are his, and none of thine
So fur as thou dost them decline:
  Come then, receive my Grace.
And when he buffits thee therefore,
If thou my aid and Grace implore,
  I'le shew a pleasant face.

But still look for Temptations Deep,
Whilst that thy Noble Sparke doth keep
  Within a Mudwald Cote.
These White Frosts and the Showers that fall
Are but to whiten thee withall,
  Not rot the Web they smote.

If in the fire where Gold is tri'de,
Thy Soule is put, and purifi'de,
  Wilt thou lament thy loss?
If silver-like this fire refine
Thy Soul and make it brighter Shine:
  Wilt thou bewaile the Dross?

Oh! fight my Field: no Colours fear:
I'l be thy Front, I'l be thy reare.
  Fail not: my Battells fight.
Defy the Tempter, and his Mock.
Anchor thy heart on mee, thy Rock.
  I do in thee Delight.

An Extasy of Joy let in by this Reply
returnd in Admiration

My Sweet Deare Lord, for thee I'le Live, Dy, Fight.
    Gracious indeed! My Front! My Rear!
    Almighty magnify a Mite?
      O! What a Wonder's here!

Had I ten thousand times ten thousand hearts:
    And Every Heart ten thousand Tongues;
    To praise, I should but stut[1] odd parts
      Of what to thee belongs.

If all the world did in Alimbeck ly,
    Bleeding its Spirits out in Sweat,
    It could not halfe enlife a Fly
      To Hum thy Praises greate.

If all can't half enlife a Fly to hum,
    (Which scarce an Animall we call)
    Thy Praises then which from me come,
      Come next to none at all.

For I have made myselfe ten thousand times
    More naught than nought itselfe, by sin.
    Yet thou extendst thy Gracious Shines
      For me to bath therein.

Oh! Stand amaizd, yee Angells Bright, come run
    Yee Glorious Heavens and Saints, to sing:
    Place yee your praises in the sun,
      Ore all the world to ring.

Nay, stand agast, ye sparkling Spirits bright!
    Shall little Clods of Dust you peere?
    Shall they toote Praises on your pipe?
      Oh! that we had it here.

What! can a Crumb of Dust sally such praise
    Which do from Earth all heaven o're ring?
Who swaddle up the suns bright rayes
    Can in a Flesh Flie's Wing?

Can any Ant stand on the Earth and spit
    Another out to peer with this?
Or Drink the Ocean up, and yet
    Its belly empty is?

Thou may'st this World as easily up hide
    Under the Blackness of thy naile:
As scape Sins Gulph without a Guide:
    Or Hell without a bale.

If all the Earthy Mass were rambd in Sacks,
    And saddled on an Emmets small,
Its Load were light unto those packs
    Which Sins do bring on all.

But sure this burden'd Emmet moves no wing.
    Nay, nay, Compar'd with thee, it flies.
Yet man is easd his weight of Sin:
    From hell to Heaven doth rise.

When that the World was new, its Chiefe Delight
    One Paradise alone Contain'de.
The Bridle of Mans Appetite
    The Appletree refrain'de.

The which he robbing, eat the fruit as good,
    Whose Coare hath Chokd him and his race.
And juyce hath poyson'd all their blood;
    He's in a Dismall Case.

None can this Coare remove, Poyson expell:
    He, if his Blood ben't Clarifi'de
Within Christs veans, must fry in Hell,
    Till God be satisfi'de.

Christ to his Father saith, 'Incarnate make
   Mee, Mee, thy Son; and I will doe't:
   I'le purify his Blood, and take
     The Coare out of his Throate'

All this he did, and did for us, vile Clay:
   Oh! let our Praise his Grace assaile.
   To free us from Sins Gulph each way,
     He's both our Bridge and Raile.

Although we fall and Fall and Fall and Fall,
   And Satan fall on us as fast:
   He purgeth us and doth us call
     Our trust on him to Cast.

My Lumpish Soul, why art thou hamper'd thus,
   Within a Crumb of Dust? Arise,
   Trumpet out Praises! Christ for us
     Hath slain our Enemies.

Screw up, Deare Lord, upon the highest pin
   My soul, thy ample Praise to sound.
   O tune it right, that every string
     May make thy praise rebound.

But oh! how slack, slow, dull? with what delay
   Do I this Musick to, repare,
   While tabernacled in clay
     My Organs Cottag'de are?

Yet, Lord, accept this Pittance of thy praise,
   Which as a Traveller I bring,
   While travelling along thy wayes,
     In broken notes I sing.

And at my journies end in endless joyes
   I'l make amends where Angells meet
   And sing their flaming Melodies
     In Ravishing tunes most Sweet.

The Second Ranke Accused

You that are branded for Rebellion,
What whimsy Crotchets do you feed upon?
Under my Flag you fighting, did Defie
And Vend much Venom spit at God most high:
You dar'de him as a Coward, out, and went
Flinging your Poyson'd darts against his tent.
When Grace did sound her parle, you stopt the Eare:
You backward drew, as she to you drew neere.
But whats this Grace, which you, forsooth, so prize,
For which you stand your own Sworn Enemies?
Whoever saw, smelt, tasted, felt the same?
It's but an airy notion, or a name:
Fine food for fools, or shallow brains, who know
No better fair, and therefore let all go.
Did mercy better Cain, or make him thrive,
When he pronounc'd himselfe a Fugitive:
What Benefit had Esau who did weep,
And in Repenting, teares did scald his Cheek?
Or what King Ahab, that he softly went?
Or what poore Judas that he did repent?
Grace doom'd them down to hellish flames, although
To Court the same they steep't their Souls in woe.
To whom she yields a smile, she doth expect
That with a smile, her smile they soon accept:
But you have hitherto like sturdy Clowns
Affronted Grace, and paid her Smiles with Frowns.
Nay, Mercy lookes before she Gives, to see
That those to whom she gives, true Christians bee:
That all the Graces of the Spirit do
Like Clouds of Sweet perfume from such forth flow;
And that their Souls be to the spirits feet
An Aromatick Spicery most Sweet.
Is't so with you? You from her scepter fly,
As judging it a grace graceless to dy.
Your Faith's a Phancy; Fear a Slavery.
Your Hope is Vain, Patience Stupidity.

Your Love is Carnall, selfish, set on toyes:
Your Pray'res are Prattle, or Tautologies.
Your Hearts are full of sins both Small and Greate:
They are as full as is an Egge of meate.
Your Holy Conference and talkings do
But for a Broken Piece of Non-Sense go.
If so, you are accurst; God doth impart
His Blessings onely on the broken heart.
But search your peace turnd o're, and view each side:
Graces magnetick touch will it abide?
Doth Mercys Sun through Peaces lattice clear
Shine in thy Soule? Then what's that Uproare there?
Look well about you, try before you trust:
Though Grace is Gracious; Justice still is just.
    If so it be with you, say what you can,
     You are not Saints, or I no Sinner am.

The Third Rank accused

What! thou art too for Christ, it seems? Yet fain
Thou wouldst the World with all her Pomps mentain.
But such as share of Christ, fall short of these,
And have but faint affections to such fees.
Go Coach thine Eyes about the world, and eye
Those Rich inchanting Braveries that Cry:
'Give us your heart'. Wherefore thy heart doth ake
That it such Amorous Objects must forsake;
The Love whereto so stuffs thy heart, no place
Is left therein for any Saving Grace.
Its folly then to think that Grace was shown,
When in persute thy heart was overthrown.
It was not Grace in Grace that made thee fall:
For unto Grace thou hast no heart at all.
Thou thoughtst these Objects of thy Love would faile:
The thoughts of which do make thy Spirits faile.
And this is easely prov'd: for thou didst goe
Into the field with God, as with a foe.
And bravely didst outbrave the Notion Grace,
And Chose to flee rather than it imbrace.
And well thou mightst. A Bird in hand doth far
Transcend the Quires that in the Hedges are.
And so its still: turn o're thy heart thou'lt finde
As formerly, so still thou art inclinde.
In sin thou hadst delight; didst grace defy:
And dost so still: For still thou dost reply.
Whoever went to Hell, and Came again
To shew to anyone, what is that pain?
Did ever any slip to Heaven to see
Whether there's there a God? and who is hee?
What is that fanci'de God rowl'd o're the tongue?
Oh! Brainsick Notion, or an Oldwifes Song!
That He should wholy be in e'ry place:
At once all here and there, yet in no space.
That all should be in any part though small:
That any part of him should be him all.

And that he hath no parts, though Head and Heart,
Hands, Ears, and Eyes he hath, he hath no part.
That he is all in all, yea, all in thee,
That he is also all that time in mee:
That he should be all in each Atom small,
And yet the whole cannot contain him all:
That he doth all things in a moment see,
At once, of things to Come, Past, and now bee:
That He no Elder, he no Younger is,
Than when the World began: (What wonder's this?)
That time that flies from all, with Him remains:
These are Chamaera's Coin'd in Wanton brains,
Among which Fopperies mans Soul may go,
Concerning which thou mak'st so much ado.
Nay; what or where is Hell? Can any show?
This Bugbear in the Darke's a mere Scare-Crow.
But say its true there is an Hell: a God;
A Soul Immortall in a mortall Clod:
Did God such principles infuse, as egge
The Soul from him into Eternall plague?
Thou dost Confess that God doth not demand
Such things of us as had are of no hand:
Which sure he doth, if he deny to save
Whom live by Natures Law: which Law he Gave.
Yet grant this tenet which thy heart denies,
Christ saveth none but whom he Sanctifies.
Thou art not Sanctifi'de in any part,
For sins keepe Centinall within thy heart:
And there they train, therein they Rentdevouz.
Her troops therein do quarter, and do house,
And hence as from a fountain Head there streams
Through ev'ry part Pollution in the Veans.
Hence sprouts Presumption making much too bold,
To catch such Shaddows which no hand can hold.
Hence Harebrain'd Rashness rustles in the Brain:
Hence Madbrain'd Anger, which no man can tame.
Hence Crackbrain'd folly, or a shatter'd Wit,
That none Can Plaster, none can med'cine it.

Hence a stiff, stubborn, and Rebellious Will,
That sooner breakes than buckles to fulfill
Gods Laws: and so for other sins thou'lt find
A Forward Will joyn'd with a froward minde.
Thy Heart doth lip such Languague, though thy Lip
Is loath to let such Languague open slip.
I see thy secret thoughts: and such they bee,
That Wish there was no God, or I was Hee;
Or that there was no Holiness, unless
Those sins thou'rt given to, were Holiness.
Or that there was no Hell, except for those
Who stand for Holiness, and sin oppose:
Or that there was no heaven t' enter in,
Except for those Who pass their Lives in Sin.
Though thou the Languague of thy heart outface
Dost, yet thou huggest sin, dost hiss out Grace:
Set Heaven and Hell aside its clearly shown,
Thou lov'st mee more than God thou seem'st to own.
Hence was it not for these, it plainly 'pears
Thy God for servants might go shake his ears.
For thou to keep within my booke, dost still
Ungod thy God, not walking by his Will.
    This Languague of thy heart doth this impart:
    I am a Saint, if thou no Sinner art.

A Threnodiall Dialogue between The Second and Third Ranks

SECOND

Oh you! How do you? Alas! how do things go
With you, and with your Souls? For once we know
You did as we, Welt, Wallow, Soake in Sin;
For which Gods ire infires our hearts within.

THIRD

Ne're worse, though when secure in sin much worse.
Though curst by sin, we did not feele the Curse.
Now seing we no help can see, we rue;
Would God it was with us as't is with you.

SECOND

With us! alas! a Flint would melt to see
A Deadly foe in such [a] Case as wee.
God seems our Foe, repent we Can't: but finde
To ill Goodwill; to Good, a wayward minde.

THIRD

This is't in you your Grace, we easely spie
The Love of God within your looks to ly.
But oh! our Souls set in sins Cramp, stand bent
To Badness, and not Grace we have t' Repent.

SECOND

This is your Charity. But if you saw
Those ugly Crawling Sins that do us knaw,
You'd Change your minde. You mourn and pray, we see:
We would not for a World you were as wee.

THIRD

Repent! and Pray! Aye, so the Traytor Cast
Cries, *Good my Lord!* yea, when his Doom is past.
You erre through your Abundant Charity.
We dare not wish, as we, our Enemy.

73

SECOND

Your Low esteemings of yourselves enlarge
Ours of you much. But oh, that Dismall Charge!
We don't Repent, Believe, we nothing do:
No Grace we have, though something Gracelike show.

THIRD

Is't so with you who do so much outdo
Poor nothings us? Oh! whither shall we go?
Our Grace a Mockgrace is: of Ulcerous Boiles.
We are as full, as Satan is of Wiles.

SECOND

There's not a Sin that is not in our Heart,
And if Occasion were, it would out start.
There's not a Precept that we have not broke,
Hence not a Promise unto us is spoke.

THIRD

Its worse with us: The Preacher speaks no word,
The Word of God no sentence doth afford;
But fall like burning Coals of Hell new blown
Upon our Souls, and on our Heads are thrown.

SECOND

Its worse with us. Behold Gods threatonings all;
Nay, Law and Gospell on our Heads do fall.
Both Hell and Heaven, God and Divell Do
With Wracking Terrours Consummate our Woe.

THIRD

We'le ne're believe that you are worse than wee,
For Worse than us wee judge no Soul can bee.
We know not where to run, nor what to doe:
Would God it was no worse with us than you.

SECOND

Than us alas! what, would you fain aspire
Out of the Frying Pan into the Fire?[1]

Change States with you with all our hearts we would;
Nay, and give boot therewith, if that we could.

THIRD

Say what you can, we can't but thinke this true,
That Grace's Ambush hath surprized you.
But Judgment layes an Ambush strong to take
[   ]¹

SECOND

What Charity have you for us? When thus
You judge amiss both of yourselves and us?
What pitty is't? Yet God will you repay.
Although we perish, and be cast away.

THIRD

The Lord forbid the last, and grant we may
Deceived be wherein we be, you say.
We Cannot wish a Toade as wee: but Crave
Your prayers for us, that we may pardon have.

SECOND

Our Pray'res are pray'reless: Oh! to what we bee,
An ugly Toad's an Angell bright we see.
Oh pray, pray you, oh pray, for us that so
The Lord of Mercy Mercy on's may show.

THIRD

O would we could! but oh Hells Gripes do grinde;
Yea, writh our Souls with Cramps of e'ry kinde.
If Grace begrace us not, we go to Hell:
The Good Lord help us both, thus fare you Well.

Their Call in this Sad State for Mercy

We humbly beg, oh Lord, to know our Crime:
That we thus tortur'de are before our time.
Before our time? Lord, give's this Word again,
For we have long ago deserv'de Hells flame.
If Mercy wrought not Miracles, none could
Us monuments of mercy now behold.
But oh! while Mercy waits, we slave to sin,
Heap up sins Epha far above the brim.
What shall we do when to account we're Calld?
How will abused Mercy burn and scald?
We know not How nor Where to stay or goe.
We know not whom nor What to trust or doe.
Should we run hence from Mercy, Justice will
Run hotly after us our blood to spill.
But should we run to Mercy, Justice may
Hold Mercies hands while Vengeance doth us slay.
And if we trust to Grace, necessity
Binds us by force at Grace's Grace to ly;
But if we run from Grace, we headlong cast
Ourselves upon the Spiles[1] of Ruine Vast.
And if we claim her ours, she'l surely smite
Us, for presuming on an others right.

Who'le with a Leaking, old Crack't Hulk assay
To brave the raging Waves of Adria?
Or who can Cross the Main Pacifick o're?
Without a Vessell Wade from shore to shore?
What! wade the mighty main from brim to brim,
As if it would not reach above the Chin?
But, oh! poor wee, must wade from brinck to brinck
With such a weight as would bright Angells sink.
Or venture angry Adria, or drown
When Vengeance's sea doth break the floodgates down.
If Stay, or Go to sea, we drown. Then see
In what a wofull Pickle, Lord, we bee.
Rather than tarry, or the rough sea trust,

On the Pacificke Ocean forth we thrust.
Necessity lies on's: we dare not stay:
If drown we must, we'l drown in Mercy's Sea!
Impute it not presumption if we high
To Cast ourselves on Mercies Clemency.
Is't not as great Presumption, Lord, to stand
And gaze on ruine, but refuse the hand
Which offers help? Or on such Courses fall
Which fall to ruin, ruinating all?
Lord, pitty, pitty us, Lord, pitty send:
A thousand pitties 'tis we should offend.
But oh! we did, and are thereto propence:[1]
And what we count off, oft thou Count'st offence.
We've none to trust: but on thy Grace we ly;
If dy we must, in mercy's arms wee'l dy.

    Then pardon, Lord, and put away our guilt:
    So we be thine, deale with us as thou wilt.

The Soule Bemoning Sorrow rowling upon a resolution to Seek Advice of Gods people

Alas! my Soule, product of Breath Divine,
For to illuminate a Lump of Slime.
Sad Providence! Must thou below thus tent
In such a Cote as strangles with ill s[c]ent?
Or in such sensuall Organs make thy stay,
Which from thy noble end do make thee stray?
My nobler part, why dost thou laquy to
The Carnall Whynings of my senses so?
What? thou become a Page, a Peasant! nay,
A Slave unto a Durty Clod of Clay!
Why should the Kirnell bring such Cankers forth
To please the shell, as will devour them both?
Why didst thou thus thy Milkwhite Robes defile
With Crimson spots of scarlet sins most vile?

My Muddy Tent, why hast thou done so ill
To Court and kiss my Soule, yet kissing kill?
Why didst thou Whyning, egg her thus away,
Thy sensuall Appetite to satisfy?
Art thou so safe and firm a Cabinet,
As though thou soaking lie in nasty wet,
And in all filthy Puddles: yet the thin
Can ne're drench through to stain the Pearle within?
Its no such thing! Thou'rt but a Cawle-wrought Case,
And when thou fallst, thou foulst its shining face;
Or but her mudwalld Lid which wet by sin,
Diffuseth all in her that [enters?] in.
One stain stains both, when both in one Combine:
A Musty Cask doth marre rich Malmsy Wine.

Woe's mee! my mouldering Heart! What must I do?
When is my moulting time to shed my woe?
Oh! Woefull fall! what, fall from Heavenly bliss
To th' bottom of the bottomless Abyss?
Above, an angry God! Below, black-blue

Brimstony flames of hell where Sinners rue!
Behinde, a Traile of Sins! Before appeare
An Host of Mercies that abused were!
Without, a Raging Divell! and Within,
A Wracking Conscience Galling home for Sin!
What! Canst not finde one Remedy, my Soule,
On Mercies File for mee? Oh! Search the Rowle.
What! freeze to death under such melting means,
Of Grace's Golden, Life-Enliv'ning Beams?
What? not one Hope? Alas! I hope there's some,
Although I know not in what way it come.
Although there is no hope within my minde,
I'le force Hope's Faculty, till Hope I find.
Some glimmerings of Hope, I hope to spy
In Mercies Golden Stacks, or Remedy.
I therefore am Resolv'd a search to make,
And of the Pious Wise, some Counsill take.
Ile then in Pensiveness myselfe apply
To them in hope, but yet halfe hopelessly.
Perhaps these thoughts are blessed motions, though
From whence they are, as yet I do not know.
    And if from Christ, Oh, then thrice Happy mee!
    If not, I'st not be worser than I bee.

The Preface

[SOUL]
Long lookt for Sir! Happy, right Happy Saint!
I long to lay before you my Complaint,
And gain your Counsill: but you're strange. And I
Through backwardness lost opportunity.

SAINT
How is't, good Sir! Methinks I finde there dart
Some pleasant Hopes of you within my heart.
What, is your Rantery declinde, foregone?
Your looks are like the Earth you tread upon.

SOUL
It's true. I do, and well may look so, too,
For worse than mee the world did never show.
My sins are di'de in grain: all Grace I lack.
This doth my Soul on tenterhooks enwrack.
Wherefore I Counsill Crave touching my sin,
My Want of Grace; Temptations too within.

The Souls Doubts touching its Sins Answerd

SAINT

It this thy Case, Poor Soul? Come then begin:
Make known thy griefe: anatomize thy sin.
Although thy sins as Mountains vast do show,
Yet Grace's fountain doth these mountains flow.

SOUL

True, true indeed, where Mountains sinke, but where
The[y] swim, their Heads above these mountains peare.
Mine swim in Mercies boundless Ocean do:
Therefore their Heads above these waters goe.

SAINT

I thought as you, but loe! the Lyon hee
Is not so fierce as he is feign'd to bee.
But grant they swim, they'l then swim quite away
On Mercies main, if you Repenting stay.

SOUL

I swim in Mercy: but my sins are sayles
That waft my barke to Hell by Graces Gales.
Is't possible for such as Grace outbrave
(Which is my Case), true Saving Grace to have?

SAINT

That's not thy Sin: thou didst not thus transgress;
Thy Grace-outbraveing sin is bashfulness.
Thou art too backward. Satan strives to hold
Thee fast hereby, and saith, thou art too bold.

SOUL

Alas! How are you out in mee; behold,
My best is poison in a Box of Gold.
If with mine Eyes you saw my hearts black stain,
You'de judge my Sins were double di'de in grain.

SAINT

Deluded Soul, Satan beguiles thee so,
Thou judgst the bend, the back side of the bow:
Dost press thyselfe too hard: Straite wands appeare
Crook't in and out, in running rivlets Clear.

SOUL

You raise the fabrick of your pious hope
Upon such water Bells, as rots denote.
For my Profession doth but cloake my sin:
A guilded Maukin's[1] stufft with Chaff within.

SAINT

I love not thus to row in such a Stream:
And if I did, I should so touch my Theme.
But muster up your Sins, though more or few:
Grace hath an Edge to Cut their bonds atwo.

SOUL

This is my Sin: My Sin I love, but hate
God and his Grace. And who's in such a state?
My Love and Hatred do according rise
Unto Sins height, and unto Grace's sise.

SAINT

I thought as you when first to make me see,
God powred out his Spirit sweet on mee.
But oh, strange Fetch! What! Love, yet hate to have?
And hate in heart what heartily you Crave?

SOUL

Sometimes meethinks I wish, Oh! that there were
No Heaven nor Hell. For then I need not feare.
I'm pestred with black thoughts of Blasphemy,
And after thoughts do with these thoughts Comply.

SAINT

See Satans Wiles: while thou in sin didst dwell,

Thou Calledst not in Question Heaven or Hell.
But now thou'rt out with sin, he makes thee Call
In Question both, that thou in Hell mightst fall.

SOUL

But, oh! methinks, I finde I sometimes wish
There was no God, or that there was not this;
Or that his wayes were other than they bee!
Oh! Horrid, horrid, Hellish thoughts in mee!

SAINT

'Twas thus, or worse with me. I often thought,
Oh! that there was no God: or God was Naught!
Or that his Wayes were other Wayes! Yet hee
In mighty mercy hath bemerci'de mee.

SOUL

My Heart is full of thoughts, and ev'ry thought
Full of Sad, Hellish drugstery enwrought.
Methinks it strange to Faith that God should bee
Thus All in All, yet all in Each part. See.

SAINT

'Twas so with me. Then let your Faith abound,
For Faith will stand where Reason hath no ground.
This proves that God is Onely God; for hee
Surpasseth the superlative degree.

SOUL

Methinks I am a Frigot fully fraught,
And stoughed full with each Ath'istick thought.
Methinks I hate to think on God: anone
Methinks there is no God to thinke upon.

SAINT

I thought as much at first: my thoughts, so vain,
Were thus: that God was but stampt i' th' brain.
But God disperst these Wicked thoughts. Behold
The various methods of the serpent old!

SOUL

All arguments against mee argue still:
I see not one bespeaks me right, but ill.
Whatse're I use I do abuse: Oh! shew
Whether the Case was ever thus with you.

SAINT

It was: But see how Satan acts; for his
He troubles not with such a thought as this.
But Wicked thoughts he in the Saints doth fling,
And saith they're theirs, accusing them of Sin.

SOUL

Methinks my heart is harder than a flint;
My Will is Wilfull frowardness within't:
And mine Affections do my Soule betray,
Sedaning of it from the blessed way.

SAINT

Loe, Satan hath thy thoughts inchanted quite,
And Carries them a pickpack from the right:
Thou art too Credulous: For Satan lies.
It is not as you deem: deem otherwise.

SOUL

But I allow of sin: I like it well.
And Chiefly grieve, because it goes to hell.
And were it ever so with you, I see
Grace hath prevented you: which doth not mee.

SAINT

I thought as you: but now I clearly spy,
These Satans brats will like their Curst Sire ly.
He squibd these thoughts in you, you know not how,
And tempts you then to deem you them allow.

SOUL

And so I do: would I could Sins disown:
But if I do, they'l own me for their own.

I have no Grace to do't: this prooves me in
A Lamentable State, a State of Sin.

SAINT

What ambling work within a Ring is here?
What Circular Disputes of Satans Geer?
To proove thee Graceless, he thy sins persues:
To proove thee sinfull, doth thy Grace accuse.
    Why dost thou then believe the Tempter so?
    He seeks by helping thee thy Overthrow.

Doubts from the Want of Grace Answerd

SOUL

Such as are Gracious grow in Grace, therefore
Such as have Grace, are Gracious evermore.
Who sin Commit are sinfull: and thereby
They grow unglody. So I feare do I.

SAINT

Such as are Gracious, Graces have, therefore
They evermore desire to have more.
But such as never knew this dainty fare
Do never wish them 'cause they dainties are.

SOUL

Alas! alas! this still doth me benight.
I've no desire, or no Desire aright:
And this is Clear: my Hopes do witherd ly;
Before their buds breake out, their blossoms dy.

SAINT

When fruits do thrive, the blossom falls off quite:
No need of blossoms when the seed is ripe.
The Apple plainly prooves the blossoms were.
Thy withred Hopes hold out Desires as Cleare.

SOUL

Alas! my Hopes seem but like blasted fruit:
Dead on the Stoole before it leaves its root.
For if it lively were, a growth it hath,
And would be grown e're this to Saving Faith.

SAINT
[   ]¹
[   ]
Which lively is, layes hold on Christ too, though
Thou deemst it doth like blasted blossoms show.

86

SOUL

If it was so, then Certainly I should
With Faith Repentance have. But oh! behold,
This Grace leaves not in mee a single print:
Mine Eyes are Adamant, my Heart is Flint.

SAINT

Repentance is not argued so from Tears,
As from the Change that in the Soul appears,
And Faith Ruld by the Word. Hence ever spare
To mete Repentance out by Satans square.

SOUL

I fear Repentance is not Genuine:
Its Feare that makes me from my sins decline.
And if it was, I should delight much more,
To bathe in all Gods Ordinances pure.

SAINT

And dost thou not? Poore Soule, thou dost I know.
Why else dost thou Relent, and sorrow so?
But Satan doth molest thee much to fling
Thee from thy Dutie into e'ry Sin.

SOUL

If these were my Delight, I should Embrace
The royall Retinue of Saving Grace:
Peace, Patience, Pray're, Meekness, Humility,
Love, Temp'rance, Feare, Syncerety, and Joy.

SAINT

You do, though not alike at all times sure;
And you do much desire to have more.
I wonder that you judge them worth the having,
Or Crave them, if they are not got by Craving.

SOUL

My measure is so small; I doubt, alas!

It's next to none, and will for nothing pass.
But if I had but this or that Degree
Of all these Graces, then thrice Happy mee!

SAINT

You have not what you Would, and therefore will
Not own you have at all. What! Sullen still?
If God should fill you, and not work your bane,
You would not be Content, but would Complain.

SOUL

What, must my vessell voide of Grace be thrust
By you in Glory thus among the just
As Gracious, though the Dose of Grace I finde
Is scarce a Grain? Can this Content your minde?

SAINT

God, and His All's the Object of the Will:
All God alone can onely it up fill.
He'd kill the Willer, if he Will he should
Fill to the brim, while Cabbined in mould.
What Mortall can contain immortall bliss,
If it be poured on him as it is?
A single Brim thus touching him would make
The stoutest mortall man to ashes shake.
Will nothing give Content unless you have,
While here a mortall, all your Will can Crave?
If so, the Promise which is made to those
That hunger after Righteousness you'l lose.
For being full, you could not hunger still,
Nor wish for more, you having once your Will.
You cant contain Halfe what in truth you would,
Or do not Wish for Halfe of what you should.
Can't all the sea o'refill an Acorn bole?
Can't God orefill a little Whimpring Soul?
What! Can a Nutshell all the World Enfold?
Or can thy Heart all Heavens Glory Hold?
And never breake? What! Canst thou here below

Weld Heavens bliss while mortall thus? Oh! no.
God Loves you better than to grant your Cry,
When you do Cry for that which will destroy.
Give but a Child a Knife to still his Din:
He'l cut his Fingers with it ere he blin.[1]

SOUL

Had I but any Sparke of Grace, I might
Have much more than I have with much delight.
How can I trust to you? You do not know
Whether I have a Grain of Grace, or no.

SAINT

You think you might have more: you shall have so,
But if you'd all at once, you could not grow.
And if you could not grow, you'd grieving fall:
All would not then Content you, had you all.
Should Graces Floodgate thus at once breake down,
You most would lose, or else it you would drown.
He'l fill you but by drops, that so he may
Not drown you in't, nor cast a Drop away.

Doubts from Satans Temptations Answered

SOUL

But oh, the Tempter harries me so fast,
And on me falls to make me fall at last.
Had I but Grace, surely I might repell
His firy Darts that dart in fire from hell.

SAINT

If you had none, he never would bestow
Such darts upon you, Grace to overthrow.
The Bullets shot are blinde, the fowlers eye
Aims at the marke before he lets them fly.

SOUL

But he bewilders me: I scarce can finde,
But lose, myselfe again within my minde;
My thoughts are Laberryntht, I can't enjoyn
Any thereof the rest to discipline.

SAINT

I once was thus. The Crooked Serpent old
Doth strive to hinder what he can't withhold.
And where he cannot keep from Grace, he's loath
To keep from keeping Saving Grace from Growth.

SOUL

But if a Pious thought appeare, I finde
It's brambled in the briers of my minde;
Or in those brambles lost, or slinks away.
But Viprous thoughts do in these thickets stay:
With these I pest'red am in duty so,
I doubt I undo all thereby I do.

SAINT

First, Satan envies each Choice thought; then hee
To murder it, or make't short winded bee,
Doth raise a Fog, or fude[1] of thoughts most vile
Within the soul, and darkens all that ile.

90

And when he cannot hinder pray're, he'll strive
To spoil the same: but still hold on, and thrive.

SOUL

But yet I feare there oft lurks secretly
Under each Duty done, Hypocrisy.
I finde no heart unto the wayes of Grace:
It's but their End my heart would fain imbrace.

SAINT

Why give you Credit to your deadly foe?
He turns ore e'ry stone Grace t'overthrow.
He'l fight on both sides Grace, Grace to destroy:
To ruinate your Soule Eternally.
He makes some thus red mad on mischiefe grow,
And not to matter what they say, or do.
He makes Civility[1] to pass for Grace,
With such as hunt riches hot-s[c]enting trace.
To such as God doth Call, he doth reply
That all their Grace is but Hypocrisy.

    Contrarily, a Refuge strong to make
For e'ry sin, he doth this method take:
He tells the Doubting soul, this is no sin:
Untill he Diveth over head therein.
But then to breake his Heart, he doth reply
That done is Sin. He sinned willingly.
He to the Sinner saith, Great sins are small;
Small sins, he telleth him, are none at all.
And so to such there is no sin: for why
Great sins are small, Small None: but oh! but eye
If God awakes a Soul, he doth begin
To make him count indifferent things as sin:
Nay, Lawfull things wanting a Circumstance,
Or having one too much, although by Chance.
And thus he doth involve the doubting soule
In dismall doubts, and makes it fear to rowle
Himselfe on Christ for fear it should presume.
But if he doth, he quickly turns his tune,

And doth accuse, because he did not take,
As soon as mercy did an offer make.
Oh! see the Craft the Serpent old doth use
To hopple souls in Sin, and Sin to Choose.
One while he terms true Grace a morall thing;
One while morality a Splendid Sin.

SOUL

You shew the matter as the matter is,
But shew me how in such a Case as this:
T'repell the Tempter, and the field t'obtain;
To Chaff away the Chaff, and Choose the grain.

SAINT

Perform the Duty, leave th'event unto
His grace that doth both in and outside know.
Beg pardon for your Sins: bad thoughts defy,
That are Cast in you by the Enemy.
Approove yourselfe to God, and unto his,
And beg a pardon where you do amiss.
If wronged, go to God for right, and pray
Hard-thoughted Saints black-thoughted thoughts away.[1]
Renew your acts of Faith: believe in him
Who died on the Cross to Cross out Sin.
Allow not any Sin, but if you sin
Through frailty, Faith will a new pardon bring.
Do all Good Works, work all good things you know,
As if you should be sav'd for doing so.
Then undo all you've done, and it deny,
And on the naked Christ alone rely.
Believe not Satan, Unbelieve his tales
Lest you should misbelieve the Gospell bales.
    Do what is right, and for the right Contend;
    Make Grace your way, and Glory'l be your End.

Yet as a further Caution still I'le shew
You other Wiles of Satan to eschue;
And that a Saint may of a Saint account,
Not as a Saint, though once with God in th' mount.

92

Some of Satans Sophestry

The Tempter greatly seeks, though secretly,
   With an Ath'istick Hoodwinke man to blinde,
That so the footsteps of the Deity
   Might stand no longer stampt upon his minde:
   Which, when he can't blot out by blinding quite,
   He strives to turn him from the Purer Light.

With Wiles enough he on his thoughts intrudes,
   That God's a Heape of Contradictions high;
But when these thoughts man from his thoughts excludes,
   Thou knowst not then (saith he) this Mystery.
   And when the first String breaks, he strives to bring
   Into sins brambles by the other string.

When God Calls out a Soule, he subtilly
   Saith God is kinde: you need not yet forsake
Your Sins: but if he doth, he doth reply,
   Thou'st outstood Grace: Justice will vengeance take.
   He'l tell you you Presume on Grace, to fright
   You to despare, beholding Justice bright.

Though just before mans mountain sins were mites,
   His mites were nothing. Now the scales are turn'd.
His mites are mountains now of mighty height,
   And must with Vengeance-Lightening be burn'd.
   Greate Sins are Small, till men repent of Sin:
   Then Small are far too big to be forgi'n.

While man thinks slightly, that he will repent,
   There's time enough (saith he), it's easly done.
But when repent he doth, the time is spent,
   Saith he, it is too late to be begun.
   To keep man from't, it's easly done, saith he,
   To dant him in't, he saith, it Cannot bee.

So Faith is easy till the Soule resolves
   To live to Christ, and upon Christ rely.

Then Saving Faith he bold presumption Calls.
   Hast thou (saith he) in Christ propriety?
   The Faithfulls Faith, he stiles Presumption great,
   But the Presumptuous, theirs is Faith Compleat.

Nay, though the Faith be true, he acts so sly,
   As to raise doubts: and then it must not do:
Unless Assurance do it Certify:
   Which if it do, it dou[b]ts of it also.
   Faith is without Assurance shuffled out,
   And if Assurance be, that's still a Doubt.

But should the Soule assured once, once Doubt,
   Then his Assurance no Assurance is:
Assurance doth assure the Soul right out;
   Leaves not a single Doubt to do amiss.
   But Satan still will seeke to Pick an hole
   In thy Assurance to unsure thy Soul.

Should any Soule once an Assurance get
   Into his hands, soon Satans Pick-Lock key
With Sinfull Wards Unlocks his Cabinet
   To Steal the Jewell in it, thence away.
   The Soul thus pillag'de, droops unto the grave:
   It's greater griefe to lose than not to have.

He doth molest the Soule; it cannot see
   Without Assurance Extraordinary:
Which should it have, it would soon take to bee
   A Mere Delusion of the Adversary.
   Assurance would not serve, should God Convay
   It in an Usuall or Unusuall way.

Thus I might search, Poor Soul, the Magazeen
   Of Gospell Graces over: I might paint
Out Satans sculking, each side each unseen,
   To Hoodwinck Sinners, and to hopple Saints.
   For he to dim their Grace, and slick up sin,
   Calls Brass bright Gold, bright Gold but brass or tin.

He tempts to bring the soul too low or high,
 To have it e're in this or that extream:
To see no want or want alone to eye:
 To keep on either side the golden mean.
 If it was in't, to get it out he'l 'ledge
 Thou on the wrong side art the Pale or Hedge.

When God awakes a Soule, he'l seeke to thrust
 It on Despare for want of Grace, or get
And puff't with Pride, or in Security hush't,
 Or Couzen it with Graces Counterfe[i]t:
 Which if he can't, he'l Carp at Grace, and raile,
 And say, this is not Grace: it thus doth faile.

And thus he strives with Spite, Spleen, bitter Gall,
 That Sinners might Dishonour God Most high:
That Saints might never honour God at all;
 That those in Sin, these not in Grace might dy;
 And that the Righteous, Gracious, Pious, Grave,
 Might have no Comfort of the Grace they have.

Lest you be foild herewith, watch well unto
 Your Soul, that thrice Ennobled noble Gem.
For Sins are flaws therein, and double woe
 Belongs thereto if it be found in them.
 Are Flaws in Venice Glasses bad? What in
 Bright Diamonds? What then in man is Sin?

Difficulties arising from Uncharitable Cariages of Christians

When these assaults proove vain, the Enemy
   One Saint upon another oft doth set,
To make each fret like to Gum'd Taffity,
   And fire out Grace thus by a Chase or Fret.
   Uncharitable Christians inj'rous are:
   Two Freestones rubd together each do ware.

When Satan jogs the Elbow of the one
   To Spleenish Passions, which too oft doth rise,
For want of Charity, or hereupon
   From some Uncharitable harsh Surmise,
   Then the Poore Doubting Soul is oft oppresst
   By hard Reflections from an harder breast.

Th' Uncharitable Soul oft thus reflects,
   After each Birth a second birth doth Come.
Your Second Birth no Second Birth ejects:
   The Babe of Grace then's strangld in the Womb.
   There's no new Birth born in the Soul, thou'lt find,
   If that the after Birth abide behinde.

The Babe of Grace, thinks he, 's not born, its sure;
   Sins Secundine is not as yet out Cast.
The Soul no Bracelet of Graces pure
   Doth ware, while wrapt in nature's slough so fast.
   And thus he doth for want of Charity,
   The wounded wound Uncharitably.

And thus some Child of God, when led awry
   By Satan, doth with Satan take a part
Against some Child of God, whom frowardly
   He by Reflections harsh wounds thus in heart.
   Pough! Here's Religion! Strange indeed! Quoth hee,
   Grace makes a Conscience of things here that bee.

Grace Conscious makes one, how to spend ones time,
   How to perform the Duties of one's place:
Not onely in the things which are Divine,
   But in the things which ware a Sublime Face.
   Do you do so? And order good persue?
   Don't Earth and Heaven interfer in you?

Will God accept the service if the time
   Is stolen from our Calling, him to pay?
What! will he yield that Sacrifice his shine,
   That from anothers Altar's stole away?
   God and our Callings Call: and th' Sacrifice
   Stole from our Callings Altar he defies.

Yet if it falls on worldly things intense,
   It's soon scourgd then with whips of Worldliness;
It gives to many, nay, to all, offence,
   And gathers to itselfe great penciveness.
   Intense on God, or on the world: all's one;
   The Harmless Soule is hardly thought upon.

Such Traps and Wilds as these are, Satan sets
   For to intrap the Innocent therein:
These are his Wyers, Snares, and tangling Nets,
   To hanck and hopple harmless souls in sin.
   If in such briars thou enbrambled light,
   Call on the Mighty God with all thy might.

On God in Christ Call hard: For in him hee
   Hath Bowells melting, and Expanded arms:
Hath sweet imbraces, Tender mercy, free;
   Hath Might Almighty too to save from harms.
   Into his Dove streak't Downy bosom fly,
   In spit[e] of spite, or spiters Enmity.

These are Gods Way-Marks thus inscrib'd; this hand
   Points you the way unto the Land Divine,
The Land of Promise, Good Immanuels Land,

To New Jerusalem above the line.
Ten thousand times thrice tribled blesst he is,
That walketh in the suburbs here of bliss.

His Wildred state will wane away, and hence
    These Crooked Passages will soon appeare:
The Curious needlework of Providence,
    Embrodered with golden spangles Cleare.
    Judge not this Web while in the Loom, but stay
    From judging it untill the judgment day.

For while it's foiled up, the best Can see
    But little of it, and that little too
Shews weather beaten: but when it shall bee
    Hung open all at once, Oh, beautious shew!
    Though thrids run in and out, cross snarle and twin'de
    The Web will even be enwrought you'l finde.

If in the golden Meshes of this Net,
    (The Checkerwork of Providence) you're Caught,
And Carri'de hence to Heaven, never fret:
    Your Barke shall to an Happy Bay be brought.
    You'l se[e] both Good and Bad drawn up hereby;
    These to Hells Horrour, those to Heavens Joy.

Fear not Presumption then, when God invites:
    Invite not Fear, when that he doth thee Call:
Call not in Question whether he delights
    In thee, but make him thy Delight, and all.
    Presumption lies in Backward Bashfulness,
    When one is backward, though a bidden Guest.

The Effect of this Discourse upon the second and third Rancks

RANK TWO

Whence Come these Spicy Gales? Shall we abuse
   Such sweet Perfumes with putrid noses?
Who did in this Diffusive Aire Diffuse
   Such Aromatick fumes or Posies?
These Spirits are with Graces sweetly splic'te;
What Good Comes in them? Oh! they Come from Christ!

RANK THREE

Whence Come these Cloudy Pillars of Perfume?
   Sure Christ doth on his Garden blow,
Or open Graces Spice Box, I presume,
   From whence these Reechs do flow:
For oh! heart Ravishing steams do scale my Soule,
And do in Heavenly Raptures it enrowle.

RANK TWO

Sure Grace a progress in her Coach doth ride,
   Lapt up in all Perfumes, whose s[c]ent
Hath suffocated sin, and nullifi'de
   Sad Griefe, as in our Souls it went.
Sin sincks the Soul to Hell: but here is Love
Sincks Sin to Hell; and soars the Soul above.

RANK THREE

I strove to soar on high. But oh! methought
   Like to a Lump of Lead my sin
Prest down my Soul: But now it's off, she's Caught
   In holy Raptures up to him.
Oh! let us then sing Praise: methinks I soar
Above the stars, and stand at Heavens Doore.

Should all the World so wide to atoms fall,
    Should th' Aire be shred to motes; should we
    Se[e] all the Earth hackt here so small
        That none Could smaller bee?
Should Heaven and Earth be Atomizd, we guess
The Number of these Motes were numberless.

But should we then a World each Atom deem,
    Where dwell as many pious men
    As all these Motes the world Could teem,
        Were it shred into them?
Each Atom would the World surmount, wee guess,
Whose men in number would be numberless.

But had each pious man as many Tongues
    At singing all together then
    The Praise that to the Lord belongs,
        As all these Atoms men?
Each man would sing a World of Praise, we guess,
Whose Tongues in number would be numberless.

And had each Tongue, as many Songs of Praise
    To sing to the Almighty ALL;
    As all these men have Tongues to raise
        To him their Holy Call?
Each Tongue would tune a World of Praise, we guess,
Whose songs in number would be numberless.

Nay, had each song as many Tunes most sweet,
    Or one intwisting in't as many,
    As all these Tongues have songs most meet
        Unparallelld by any?
Each song a world of Musick makes, we guess,
Whose Tunes in number would be numberless.

Now should all these Conspire in us, that we
    Could breath such Praise to thee, Most High:

Should we thy Sounding Organs be
    To ring such Melody?
Our Musick would the World of Worlds outring,
Yet be unfit within thine Ears to ting.

Thou didst us mould, and us new mould when wee
    Were worse than mould we tread upon.
    Nay, Nettles made by Sin wee bee:
        Yet hadst Compassion.
Thou hast pluckt out our Stings; and by degrees
Hast of us, lately Wasps, made Lady-Bees.

Though e're our Tongues thy Praises due can fan,
    A Weevle with the World may fly,
    Yea fly away: and with a span
        We may out mete the sky.
Though what we can is but a Lisp, we pray
Accept thereof. We have no better pay.

The Soule Seeking Church-Fellowship

The Soul refresht with gracious Steams, behold,
   Christs royall Spirit richly tended
With all the guard of Graces manifold
   Throngs in to solace it amended
   And by the Trinity befriended.

Befriended thus! It lives a Life indeed.
   A Life! as if it Liv'd for Life,
For Life Eternall: wherefore with all heed,
   It trims the same with Graces rife
   To be the Lambs espoused Wife.

Yea like a Bride all Gloriously arraide
   It is arrai'de, Whose dayly ware
Is an Imbrodery with Grace inlaide,
   Of Sanctuary White most Faire:
   Its drest in Heavens fashion rare.

Each Ordinance and Instrument of Grace
   Grace doth instruct are Usefull here;
They're Golden Pipes where Holy Waters trace
   Into the spirits spicebed Deare,
   To vivify what withering were.

Hence do their Hearts like Civit-Boxes sweet
   Evaporate their Love full pure,
Which through the Chincks of their Affection reech
   To God, Christ, Christians all, though more:
   To such whose Counsills made their Cure.

Hence now Christ[s] Curious Garden fenced in
   With Solid Walls of Discipline
Well wed, and watered, and made full trim:
   The Allies all Laid out by line:
   Walks for the Spirit all Divine.

Whereby Corruptions are kept out, whereby
   Corrupters also get not in,
Unless the Lyons Carkass secretly
   Lies lapt up in a Lamblike skin,
    Which Holy seems, yet's full of sin.

For on the Towers of these Walls there stand
   Just Watchmen Watching day and night,
And Porter[s] at each Gate, who have Command
   To open onely to the right.
    And all within may have a sight.

Whose Zeale, should it along a Channell slide
   Not banckt with Knowledg right and Good,
Nor Bottomed with Love: nor wiers ti'de
   To hinder prejudiciall Blood,
    The Currant will be full of mud.

But yet this Curious Garden richly set,
   The Soul accounts Christs Paradise
Set with Choice slips and flowers, and longs to get
   Itself set here: and by advice
    To grow herein and so rejoyce.

The Soul admiring the Grace of the Church Enters into Church-Fellowship

How is this City, Lord, of thine bespangled
   With Graces shine?
With Ordinances alli'de and inam'led,
   Which are Divine?
Wall'd in with Discipline her Gates obtaine
Just Centinalls with Love Imbellisht plain.

Hence glorious and terrible she stands;
   That Converts new
Seing her Centinalls, of all demand
   The Word to shew;
Stand gazing much between two Passions Crusht:
Desire and Feare at once, which both wayes thrust.

Thus are they wrackt. Desire doth forward screw
   To get them in,
But Feare doth backward thrust, that lies purdue,
   And slicks that Pin.
You cannot give the word, Quoth she, which though
You stumble on't, its more than yet you know.

But yet Desires Screw Pin doth not slack:
   It still holds fast.
But Fears Screw Pin thrusts back, or Screw doth Crack,
   And breaks at last.
Hence on they go, and in they enter: where
Desire Converts to joy, joy Conquours Fear.

They now encovenant with God, and His;
   They thus indent
The Charters Seals belonging unto this,
   The Sacrament.
So God is theirs avoucht, they his in Christ,
In whom all things they have, with Grace are splic'te.

Thus in the usuall Coach of Gods Decree
   They bowle and swim
To Glory bright, if no Hypocrisie
   Handed them in.
For such must shake their handmaid off, lest they
Be shakt out of this Coach, or dy in th' way.

The Glory of and Grace in the Church set out

Come now behold
Within this Knot what Flowers do grow:
Spanglde like gold:
Whence Wreaths of all Perfumes do flow.
Most Curious Colours of all sorts you shall
With all Sweet Spirits s[c]ent. Yet thats not all.

Oh! Look, and finde
These Choicest Flowers most richly sweet
Are Disciplinde
With Artificiall Angells meet.
An heap of Pearls is precious: but they shall
When set by Art Excell. Yet that's not all.

Christ's Spirit showers
Down in his Word and Sacraments
Upon these Flowers,
The Clouds of Grace Divine Contents.
Such things of Wealthy Blessings on them fall
As make them sweetly thrive. Yet that's not all.

Yet still behold!
All flourish not at once. We see
While some Unfold
Their blushing Leaves, some buds there bee:
Here's Faith, Hope, Charity in flower, which call
On yonders in the Bud. Yet that's not all.

But as they stand
Like Beauties reeching in perfume
A Divine Hand
Doth hand them up to Glories room:
Where Each in sweet'ned Songs all Praises shall
Sing all ore heaven for aye. And that's but all.

The Souls Admiration hereupon

What! I such Praises sing? How can it bee?
    Shall I in Heaven sing?
What! I that scarce durst hope to see,
    Lord, such a thing?
   Though nothing is too hard for thee,
   One Hope hereof seems hard to mee.

What! Can I ever tune those Melodies,
    Who have no tune at all?
Not knowing where to stop nor Rise,
    Nor when to Fall.
   To sing thy Praise I am unfit:
   I have not learn'd my Gam-ut yet.

But should these Praises on string'd Instruments
    Be sweetly tun'de? I finde
I nonplust am, for no Consents[1]
    I ever minde.
   My Tongue is neither Quill nor Bow:
   Nor Can my Fingers Quavers show.

But was it otherwise, I have no Kit:[2]
    Which though I had, I could
Not tune the strings, which soon would slip,
    Though others should.
   But should they not, I cannot play,
   But for an F should strike an A.

And should thy Praise upon Winde Instruments
    Sound all o're Heaven Shrill?
My Breath will hardly through such Vents
    A Whistle fill:
   Which though it should, its past my spell
   By Stops and Falls to sound it Well.

How should I then, joyn in such Exercise?
    One Sight of thee'l intice

Mine Eyes to heft: whose Extasies
    Will stob[1] my Voice.
  Hereby mine Eyes will bind my Tongue,
  Unless thou, Lord, do Cut the thong.

What use of Uselesse mee then there, poore snake?
    There Saints and Angels sing
Thy Praise in full Cariere, which make
    The Heavens to ring.
  Yet if thou wilt, thou Can'st me raise
  With Angels bright to sing thy Praise.

The Joy of Church Fellowship rightly attended

In Heaven soaring up, I dropt an Eare
   On Earth: and oh! sweet Melody!
And listening, found it was the Saints who were
   Encoacht for Heaven that sang for Joy.
    For in Christs Coach they sweetly sing,
    As they to Glory ride therein.

Oh! joyous hearts! Enfir'de with holy Flame!
   Is speech thus tasseled with praise?
Will not your inward fire of Joy contain,
   That it in open flames doth blaze?
    For in Christ[s] Coach Saints sweetly sing,
    As they to Glory ride therein.

And if a string do slip by Chance, they soon
   Do screw it up again: whereby
They set it in a more melodious Tune
   And a Diviner Harmony.
    For in Christs Coach they sweetly sing,
    As they to Glory ride therein.

In all their Acts, publick and private, nay,
   And secret too, they praise impart.
But in their Acts Divine, and Worship, they
   With Hymns do offer up their Heart.
    Thus in Christs Coach they sweetly sing,
    As they to Glory ride therein.

Some few not in; and some whose Time and Place
   Block up this Coaches way, do goe
As Travellers afoot: and so do trace
   The Road that gives them right thereto;
    While in this Coach these sweetly sing,
    As they to Glory ride therein.

FIVE POEMS

An Address to the Soul Occasioned by a Rain

Ye Flippering Soule,[1]
   Why dost between the Nippers dwell?
Not stay, nor goe. Not yea, nor yet Controle.
   Doth this doe well?
      Rise journy'ng when the skies fall weeping Showers,
      Not o're nor under th' Clouds and Cloudy Powers.

Not yea, nor noe:
   On tiptoes thus? Why sit on thorns?
Resolve the matter: Stay thyselfe or goe:
   Ben't both wayes born.
      Wager thyselfe against thy surplic'de see,
      And win thy Coate, or let thy Coate win thee.

Is this th' Effect
   To leaven thus my Spirits all?
To make my heart a Crabtree Cask direct?
   A Verjuc'te Hall?
      As Bottle Ale, whose Spirits prison'd must
      When jogg'd, the bung with Violence doth burst?

Shall I be made
   A sparkling Wildfire Shop,
Where my dull Spirits at the Fireball trade
   Do frisk and hop?
      And while the Hammer doth the Anvill pay,
      The fire ball matter sparkles e'ry way.

One sorry fret,
   An anvill Sparke, rose higher,
And in thy Temple falling, almost set
   The house on fire.
      Such fireballs drop[p]ing in the Temple Flame
      Burns up the building: Lord, forbid the same.

Upon a Spider Catching a Fly

Thou sorrow, venom Elfe:
   Is this thy play,
To spin a web out of thyselfe
   To Catch a Fly?
     For why?

I saw a pettish wasp
   Fall foule therein:
Whom yet thy whorle pins[1] did no[t hasp]
   Lest he should fling
     His sting.

But as afraid, remote
   Didst stand hereat,
And with thy little fingers stroke
   And gently tap
     His back.

Thus gently him didst treate
   Lest he should pet,
And in a froppish, aspish heate
   Should greatly fret
     Thy net.

Whereas the silly Fly,
   Caught by its leg,
Thou by the throate took'st hastily,
   And 'hinde the head
     Bite Dead.

This goes to pot, that not
   Nature doth call.
Strive not above what strength hath got,
   Lest in the brawle
     Thou fall.

This Frey seems thus to us:
    Hells Spider gets
His intrails spun to whip Cords thus,
    And wove to nets,
        And sets.

To tangle Adams race
    In's stratagems
To their Destructions, Spoil'd, made base
    By venom things,
        Damn'd Sins.

But mighty, Gracious Lord,
    Communicate
Thy Grace to breake the Cord; afford
    Us Glorys Gate
        And State.

We'l Nightingaile sing like,
    When pearcht on high
In Glories Cage, thy glory, bright:
    [Yea,] thankfully,
        For joy.

Huswifery

Make me, O Lord, thy Spin[n]ing Wheele compleat;
   Thy Holy Worde my Distaff make for mee.
Make mine Affections thy Swift Flyers neate,
   And make my Soule thy holy Spoole to bee.
   My Conversation make to be thy Reele,
   And reele the yarn thereon spun of thy Wheele.

Make me thy Loome then, knit therein this Twine:
   And make thy Holy Spirit, Lord, winde quills:
Then weave the Web thyselfe. The yarn is fine.
   Thine Ordinances make my Fulling Mills.
   Then dy the same in Heavenly Colours Choice,
   All pinkt with Varnish't Flowers of Paradise.

Then cloath therewith mine Understanding, Will,
   Affections, Judgment, Conscience, Memory;
My Words and Actions, that their shine may fill
   My wayes with glory and thee glorify.
   Then mine apparell shall display before yee
   That I am Cloathd in Holy robes for glory.

Upon Wedlock and Death of Children

A Curious Knot God made in Paradise,
  And drew it out inamled neatly Fresh.
It was the True-Love Knot, more sweet than spice,
  And set with all the flowres of Graces dress.
  Its Weddens[1] Knot, that ne're can be unti'de:
  No Alexanders Sword can it divide.

The slips here planted, gay and glorious grow:
  Unless an Hellish breath do sindge their Plumes.
Here Primrose, Cowslips, Roses, Lilies blow,
  With Violets and Pinkes that voide perfumes:
  Whose beautious leaves are lac'd with Hony Dew,
  And Chanting birds Chirp out Sweet Musick true.

When in this Knot I planted was, my Stock
  Soon knotted, and a manly flower out brake.
And after it my branch again did knot:
  Brought out another Flowre: its sweet breath'd mate.
  One knot gave tother and tothers place;
  Thence Checkling[2] Smiles fought in each others face.

But oh! a glorious hand from glory came,
  Guarded with Angells, soon did Crop this flowre,
Which almost tore the root up of the same,
  At that unlookt for, Dolesome, darksome houre.
  In Pray're to Christ perfum'de it did ascend,
  And Angells bright did it to heaven tend.

But pausing on't, this Sweet perfum'd my thought,
  Christ would in Glory have a Flowre, Choice, Prime.
And having Choice, chose this my branch forth brought.
  Lord, take't I thanke thee, thou takst ought of mine;
  It is my pledg in glory; part of mee
  Is now in it, Lord, glorifi'de with thee.

But praying o're my branch, my branch did sprout,
  And bore another manly flower, and gay,

117

And after that another, sweet brake out,
    The which the former hand soon got away.
    But oh! the torture, Vomit, screechings, groans:
    And six weeks fever would pierce hearts like stones.

Griefe o're doth flow: and nature fault would finde
    Were not thy Will my Spell, Charm, Joy, and Gem:
That as I said, I say, take, Lord, they're thine:
    I piecemeale pass to Glory bright in them.
    I joy, may I sweet Flowers for Glory breed,
    Whether thou getst them green, or lets them seed.

The Ebb and Flow

When first thou on me, Lord, wrough'st thy Sweet Print,
  My heart was made thy tinder box.
  My 'ffections were thy tinder in't:
    Where fell thy Sparkes by drops.
Those holy Sparks of Heavenly fire that came
Did ever catch and often out would flame.

But now my Heart is made thy Censar trim,
  Full of thy golden Altars fire,
  To offer up Sweet Incense in
    Unto thyselfe intire:
I finde my tinder scarce thy sparks can feel
That drop out from thy Holy flint and Steel.

Hence doubts out bud for feare thy fire in mee
  'S a mocking Ignis Fatuus,
  Or lest thine Altars fire out bee,
    It's hid in ashes thus.
Yet when the bellows of thy Spirit blow
Away mine ashes, then thy fire doth glow.

SACRAMENTAL MEDITATIONS[1]

Meditation One

What Love is this of thine, that Cannot bee
   In thine Infinity, O Lord, Confinde,
Unless it in thy very Person see
   Infinity and Finity Conjoyn'd?
   What! hath thy Godhead, as not satisfi'de,
   Marri'de our Manhood, making it its Bride?

Oh, Matchless Love! Filling Heaven to the brim!
   O'rerunning it: all running o're beside
This World! Nay, Overflowing Hell, wherein
   For thine Elect, there rose a mighty Tide!
   That there our Veans might through thy Person bleed,
   To quench those flames, that else would on us feed.

Oh! that thy love might overflow my Heart!
   To fire the same with Love: for Love I would.
But oh! my streight'ned Breast! my Lifeless Sparke!
   My Fireless Flame! What Chilly Love, and Cold?
   In measure small! In Manner Chilly! See!
   Lord, blow the Coal: Thy Love Enflame in mee.

The Experience

CANTICLES I: 3: . . . thy name is as ointment poured forth.

Oh! that I alwayes breath'd in such an aire
    As I suck't in, feeding on sweet Content!
Disht up unto my Soul ev'n in that pray're
    Pour'de out to God over last Sacrament.
      What Beam of Light wrapt up my sight to finde
      Me neerer God than ere Came in my minde?

Most strange it was! But yet more strange that shine
    Which fill'd my Soul then to the brim to spy
My nature with thy Nature all Divine
    Together joyn'd in Him that's Thou, and I.
      Flesh of my Flesh, Bone of my Bone: there's run
      Thy Godhead and my Manhood in thy Son.

Oh! that that Flame which thou didst on me Cast
    Might me enflame, and Lighten ery where.
Then Heaven to me would be less at last,
    So much of heaven I should have while here.
      Oh! Sweet though Short! I'le not forget the same.
      My neerness, Lord, to thee did me Enflame.

I'le Claim my Right: Give place ye Angells Bright.
    Ye further from the Godhead stande than I.
My Nature is your Lord; and doth Unite
    Better than Yours unto the Deity.
      Gods Throne is first and mine is next: to you
      Onely the place of Waiting-men is due.

Oh! that my Heart, thy Golden Harp might bee
    Well tun'd by Glorious Grace, that e'ry string
Screw'd to the highest pitch, might unto thee
    All Praises wrapt in sweetest Musick bring.
      I praise thee, Lord, and better praise thee would,
      If what I had, my heart might ever hold.

The Reflexion

CANTICLES II: 1: I am the rose of Sharon.

Lord, art thou at the Table Head above
   Meat, Med'cine, Sweetness, sparkling Beautys, to
Enamour Souls with Flaming Flakes of Love,
    And not my Trencher, nor my Cup o'reflow?
    Ben't I a bidden guest?[1] Oh! sweat mine Eye:
    O'reflow with Teares: Oh! draw thy fountains dry.

Shall I not smell thy sweet, oh! Sharons Rose?
    Shall not mine Eye salute thy Beauty? Why?
Shall thy sweet leaves their Beautious sweets upclose?
    As halfe ashamde my sight should on them ly?
    Woe's me! For this my sighs shall be in grain,
    Offer'd on Sorrows Altar for the same.

Had not my Soule's, thy Conduit, Pipes stopt bin
    With mud, what Ravishment would'st thou Convay?
Let Graces Golden Spade dig till the Spring
    Of tears arise, and cleare this filth away.
    Lord, let thy Spirit raise my sighings till
    These Pipes my soule do with thy sweetness fill.

Earth once was Paradise of Heaven below,
    Till inkefac'd sin had it with poyson stockt;
And Chast this Paradise away into
    Heav'ns upmost Loft, and it in Glory Lockt.
    But thou, sweet Lord, hast with thy golden Key
    Unlock[t] the Doore, and made a golden day.

Once at thy Feast, I saw thee Pearle-like stand
    'Tween Heaven and Earth, where Heavens Bright glory all
In streams fell on thee, as a floodgate and,
    Like Sun Beams through thee on the World to Fall.
    Oh! Sugar sweet then! My Deare sweet Lord, I see
    Saints Heaven-lost Happiness restor'd by thee.

Shall Heaven and Earth's bright Glory all up lie,
    Like Sun Beams bundled in the sun in thee?
Dost thou sit Rose at Table Head, where I
    Do sit, and Carv'st no morsell sweet for mee?
    So much before, so little now! Sprindge,[1] Lord,
    Thy Rosie Leaves, and me their Glee afford.

Shall not thy Rose my Garden fresh perfume?
    Shall not thy Beauty my dull Heart assaile?
Shall not thy golden gleams run through this gloom?
    Shall my black Velvet Mask thy fair Face Vaile?
    Pass o're my Faults: shine forth, bright sun; arise!
    Enthrone thy Rosy-selfe within mine Eyes.

Meditation Six

CANTICLES II: 1: I am . . . the lily of the valleys.

Am I thy gold? Or Purse, Lord, for thy Wealth;
   Whether in mine or mint refinde for thee?
Ime counted so, but count me o're thyselfe,
   Lest gold washt face, and brass in Heart I bee.
   I Feare my Touchstone touches when I try
   Mee, and my Counted Gold too overly.

Am I new minted by thy Stamp indeed?
   Mine Eyes are dim; I cannot clearly see.
Be thou my Spectacles that I may read
   Thine Image and Inscription stampt on mee.
   If thy bright Image do upon me stand,
   I am a Golden Angell[1] in thy hand.

Lord, make my Soule thy Plate: thine Image bright
   Within the Circle of the same enfoile.
And on its brims in golden Letters write
   Thy Superscription in an Holy style.
   Then I shall be thy Money, thou my Hord:
   Let me thy Angell bee, bee thou my Lord.

Meditation Seven

PSALMS XLV: 2: Grace is poured into thy lips.

Thy Humane Frame, my Glorious Lord, I spy,
    A Golden Still with Heavenly Choice drugs filld:
Thy Holy Love, the Glowing heate whereby
    The Spirit of Grace is graciously distilld.
    Thy Mouth the Neck through which these spirits still;
    My Soul thy Violl make, and therewith fill.

Thy Speech the Liquour in thy Vessell Stands,
    Well ting'd with Grace, a blessed Tincture, Loe,
Thy Words distilld Grace in thy Lips pourd, and
    Give Graces Tinctur in them where they go.
    Thy words in graces tincture stilld, Lord, may
    The Tincture of thy Grace in me Convay.

That Golden Mint of Words thy Mouth Divine
    Doth tip these Words, which by my Fall were spoild;
And Dub with Gold dug out of Graces mine,
    That they thine Image might have in them foild.
    Grace in thy Lips pourd out's as Liquid Gold:
    Thy Bottle make my Soule, Lord, it to hold.

Meditation Eight

JOHN VI: 51: I am the living bread.

I ken[n]ing through Astronomy Divine
   The Worlds bright Battlement, wherein I spy
A Golden Path my Pensill cannot line
   From that bright Throne unto my Threshold ly.
   And while my puzzled thoughts about it pore,
   I find the Bread of Life in't at my doore.

When that this Bird of Paradise put in
   This Wicker Cage (my Corps) to tweedle praise
Had peckt the Fruite forbid: and so did fling
   Away its Food, and lost its golden dayes,
   It fell into Celestiall Famine sore,
   And never could attain a morsell more.

Alas! alas! Poore Bird, what wilt thou doe?
   This Creatures field no food for Souls e're gave:
And if thou knock at Angells dores, they show
   An Empty Barrell: they no soul bread have.
   Alas! Poore Bird, the Worlds White Loafe is done,
   And cannot yield thee here the smallest Crumb.

In this sad state, Gods Tender Bowells run
   Out streams of Grace: And he to end all strife,
The Purest Wheate in Heaven, his deare-dear Son
   Grinds, and kneads up into this Bread of Life:
   Which Bread of Life from Heaven down came and stands
   Disht in thy Table up by Angells Hands.

Did God mould up this Bread in Heaven, and bake,
   Which from his Table came, and to thine goeth?
Doth he bespeake thee thus: This Soule Bread take;
   Come, Eate thy fill of this, thy Gods White Loafe?
   Its Food too fine for Angells; yet come, take
   And Eate thy fill! Its Heavens Sugar Cake.

What Grace is this knead in this Loafe? This thing
    Souls are but petty things it to admire.
Yee Angells, help: This fill would to the brim
    Heav'ns whelm'd-down Chrystall meele Bowle, yea and hi
    This Bread of Life dropt in thy mouth doth Cry:
    Eate, Eate me, Soul, and thou shalt never dy.

Meditation Twelve

ISAIAH LXIII: 1: Who is this that cometh from Edom, with dyed garments from Bozrah? this that is glorious in his apparel, travelling in the greatness of his strength? I that speak in righteousness, mighty to save.

This Quest rapt at my Eares broad golden Doores:
  Who's this that comes from Edom in this shine,
In Di'ed Robes from Bozrah? this more oer
    All Glorious in's Apparrell: all Divine?
    Then through that Wicket rusht this gust[1] there gave:
    It's I that right do speake, mighty to save.

I threw through Zions Lattice then an Eye
  Which spi'de one like a lump of Glory pure:
Nay, Cloaths of gold button'd with pearls do ly
    Like Rags, or shooclouts unto his he wore.
    Heavens Curtains blanch't with Sun, and Stars of Light
    Are black as sackcloath to his Garments bright.

One shining sun guilding the skies with Light,
  Benights all Candles with their flaming Blaze:
So doth the Glory of this Robe benight
    Ten thousand suns at once ten tho[u]sand wayes.
    For e'ry thrid therein's dy'de with the shine
    Of All, and Each the Attributes Divine.

The sweetest breath, the sweetest Violet,
  Rose, or Carnation ever did gust out,
Is but a Foist[2] to that Perfume beset
    In thy Apparell steaming round about.
    But is this so? My Peuling soul then pine
    In Love untill this Lovely one be thine.

Pluck back the Curtains, back the Window Shutts:[3]
  Through Zions Agate Window take a view,
How Christ in Pincked Robes from Bozrah puts,
  Comes Glorious in's Apparell forth to Wooe.

131

Oh! if his Glory ever kiss thine Eye,
Thy Love will soon inchanted be thereby.

Then Grieve, my Soul, thy vessell is so small,
    And holds no more for such a Lovely Hee.
That strength's so little, Love scarce acts at all;
    That sight's so dim, doth scarce him lovely see.
    Grieve, grieve, my Soul, thou shouldst so pimping bee,
    Now such a Price is here presented thee.

All sight's too little sight enough to make,
    All strength's too little Love enough to reare,
All Vessells are too small to hold or take
    Enough Love up for such a Lovely Deare.
    How little to this Little's then thy ALL,
    For Him whose Beauty saith all Love's too small?

My Lovely One, I fain would love thee much,
    But all my Love is none at all I see;
Oh! let thy Beauty give a glorious t[o]uch
    Upon my Heart, and melt to Love all mee.
    Lord, melt me all up into Love for thee,
    Whose Loveliness excells what love can bee.

Meditation Nineteen

PHILIPPIANS II: 9: Wherefore God also hath highly exalted him.

Looke till thy Looks look wan, my Soule; here's ground
   The Worlds bright Eye's dash't out: Day-Light so brave
Benighted; the sparkling sun, palde round
   With flouring Rayes, lies buri'de in its grave;
   The Candle of the World blown out, down fell
   Life knockd ahead by Death: Heaven by Hell.

Alas! This World all filld up to the brim
   With Sins, Deaths, Divells, Crowding men to Hell;
For whose reliefe Gods milkwhite[1] Lamb stept in,
   Whom those Curst Imps did worry, flesh and fell;
   Tread under foot; did Clap their Wings and so
   Like Dunghill Cocks over their Conquour'd, Crow.

Brave, Pious Fraud; as if the setting sun
   Dropt like a Ball of Fire into the seas,
And so went out. But to the East come run:
   You'l meet the morn shrin'de with its flouring Rayes.
   This Lamb in laying of these Lyons dead,
   Drank of the brooke: and so lift up his Head.

Oh! Sweet, sweet joy! These Rampant Fiends befoold:
   They made their Gall his Winding sheete; although
They of the Heart-ach dy must, or be Cool'd
   With Inflamation of the Lungs, they know.
   He's Cancelling the Bond, and making Pay:
   And Ballancing Accounts: its Reckoning day.

See, how he from the Counthouse shining went
   In Flashing Folds of Burnish't Glory, and
Dasht out all Curses from the Covenant:
   Hath Justices Acquittance in his hand;
   Pluck't out Deaths sting; the Serpents Head did mall:
   The Bars and Gates of Hell he brake down all.

The Curse thus Lodgd within his Flesh, and Clogde,
  Can't run from him to his, so much he gave.
And like a Gyant he awoke, beside:
  The Sun of Righteousness rose out of's Grave:
  And setting Foot upon its neck I sing:
  Grave, where's thy Victory? Death, where's thy sting?

Meditation Twenty

PHILIPPIANS II: 9: Wherefore God also hath highly exalted him.

View, all ye eyes above, this sight which flings
   Seraphick Phancies in Chill Raptures high:
A Turffe of Clay, and yet bright Glories King:
   From dust to Glory Angell-like to fly.
   A Mortall Clod immortaliz'de, behold,
   Flyes through the skies swifter than Angells could.

Upon the Wings he of the Winde rode in
   His Bright Sedan, through all the Silver Skies,
And made the Azure Cloud, his Charriot, bring
   Him to the Mountain of Celestiall joyes.
   The Prince o' th' Aire durst not an Arrow spend,
   While through his Realm his Charriot did ascend.

He did not in a Fiery Charriot's shine,
   And Whirlewinde, like Elias upward goe.
But th' golden Ladders Jasper rounds did climbe
   Unto the Heavens high from Earth below.
   Each step had on a Golden Stepping Stone
   Of Deity unto his very Throne.

Methinks I see Heavens sparkling Courtiers fly,
   In flakes of Glory down him to attend;
And heare Heart Cramping notes of Melody
   Surround his Charriot as it did ascend:
   Mixing their Musick, making e'ry string
   More to inravish, as they this tune sing.

God is Gone up with a triumphant shout:
   The Lord with sounding Trumpets melodies:
Sing Praise, sing Praise, sing Praise, sing Praises out,
   Unto our King sing praise seraphick-wise!
   Lift up your Heads, ye lasting Doore, they sing,
   And let the King of Glory Enter in.

Art thou ascended up on high, my Lord,
   And must I be without thee here below?
Art thou the sweetest joy the Heavens afford?
   Oh! that I with thee was! what shall I do?
   Should I pluck Feathers from an Angells Wing,
   They could not waft me up to thee my King.

Lend mee thy Wings, my Lord, I'st fly apace,
   My Soules Arms stud with thy strong Quills, true Faith;
My Quills then Feather with thy Saving Grace,
   My Wings will take the Winde thy Word displai'th.
   Then I shall fly up to thy glorious Throne
   With my strong Wings whose Feathers are thine own.

Meditation Twenty-Five

EPHESIANS V: 27: A glorious church . . .

Why should my Bells, which Chime thy Praise, when thou
   My Shew-Bread, on thy Table wast, my King,
Their Clappers, or their Bell-ropes want even now?
     Or those that can thy Changes sweetly ring?
     What! is a Scar-Fire[1] broken out? No, no.
     The Bells would backward ring if it was so.

Its true: and I do all things backward run;
   Poor Pillard,[2] I have a sad tale to tell:
My soule starke nakt, rowld all in mire, undone,
     Thy Bell may tole my passing Peale to Hell.
     None in their Winding sheet more naked stay
     Nor Dead than I. Hence oh! the Judgment Day.

When I behold some Curious Piece of Art,
   Or Pritty Bird, Flower, Star, or Shining Sun,
Poure out o'reflowing Glory: oh! my Heart
     Achs seing how my thoughts in snick-snarls[3] run.
     But all this Glory to my Lord's a spot,
     While I instead of any, am all blot.

But, my sweet Lord, what glorious robes are those
   That thou hast brought out of thy Grave for thine?
They do outshine the sun-shine, Grace the Rose:
     I leape for joy to thinke, shall these be mine?
     Such are, as waite upon thee in thy Wars,
     Cloathd with the Sun, and Crowned with twelve stars.

Dost thou adorn some thus, and why not mee?
   Ile not believe it. Lord, thou art my Chiefe.
Thou my Commandest to believe in thee:
     I'l not affront thee thus with Unbeliefe.
     Lord, make my Soule Obedient: and whenso
     Thou saist Believe, make it reply, I do.

I fain the C[h]oicest Love my soule Can get,
    Would to thy Gracious selfe a Gift present.
But cannot now unscrew Loves Cabbinet.
    Say not this is a Niggards Complement:
    For seing it is thus, I choose now rather
    To send thee th' Cabbinet and Pearle together.

Meditation Twenty-Eight

JOHN 1: 16: And of his fulness have all we received, and grace for grace.

When I, Lord, send some Bits of Glory home,
  (For Lumps I lack) my Messenger, I finde,
Bewildred, lose his way, being alone.
    In my befogg'd Dark Phancy, Clouded minde,
    Thy Bits of Glory packt in Shreds of Praise
    My Messenger doth lose, losing his Wayes.

Lord, Cleare the Coast: and let thy sweet sun shine,
  That I may better speed a second time:
Oh! fill my Pipkin[1] with thy Blood red Wine:
    I'l drinke thy Health: To pledge thee is no Crime.
    Although I but an Earthen Vessell bee,
    Convay some of thy Fulness into me.

Thou, thou my Lord, art full, top full of Grace,
  The Golden Sea of Grace: Whose springs thence come,
And Pretious Drills, boiling in ery place.
    Untap thy Cask, and let my Cup Catch some.
    Although it's in an Earthen Vessells Case,
    Let it no Empty Vessell be of Grace.

Let thy Choice Caske shed, Lord, into my Cue[2]
  A Drop of Juyce presst from thy Noble Vine.
My Bowl is but an Acorn Cup; I sue
    But for a Drop: this will not empty thine.
    Although I'me in an Earthen Vessells place,
    My Vessell make a Vessell, Lord, of Grace.

My Earthen Vessell make thy Font also:
  And let thy sea my Spring of Grace in't raise.
Spring up, oh Well! my Cup with Grace make flow.
    Thy Drops will on my Vessell ting thy Praise.
    I'l sing this Song, when I these Drops Embrace:
    My Vessell now's a Vessell of thy Grace.

Meditation Twenty-Nine

JOHN XX: 17: I ascend unto my Father, and your Father; and to my God, and your God.

My shattred Phancy stole away from mee,
  (Wits run a Wooling over Edens Parke)
And in Gods Garden saw a golden Tree,
    Whose Heart was All Divine, and gold its barke:
    Whose glorious limbs and fruitfull branches strong
    With Saints and Angells bright are richly hung.

Thou! thou! my Deare-Deare Lord, art this rich Tree:
  The Tree of Life within Gods Paradise.
I am a Withred Twig, dri'de, fit to bee
    A Chat[1] Cast in thy fire, writh off by Vice.
    Yet if thy Milkwhite Gracious Hand will take mee,
    And grafft mee in this golden stock, thou'lt make mee.

Thou'lt make me then its Fruite and Branch to spring.
  And though a nipping Eastwinde blow, and all
Hells Nymps with spite their Dog's sticks thereat ding
    To Dash the Grafft off, and its fruit to fall,
    Yet I shall stand thy Grafft, and Fruits that are
    Fruits of the Tree of Life thy Grafft shall beare.

I being grafft in thee, there up do stand
  In us Relations all that mutuall are.
I am thy Patient Pupill, Servant, and
    Thy Sister, Mother, Doove, Spouse, Son, and Heire:
    Thou art my Priest, Physician, Prophet, King,
    Lord, Brother, Bridegroom, Father, Ev'rything.

I being grafft in thee am graffted here
  Into thy Family and kindred Claim
To all in Heaven: God, Saints, and Angells there.
    I thy Relations my Relations name.
    Thy Father's mine, thy God my God, and I
    With Saints and Angells draw Affinity.

My Lord, what is it that thou dost bestow?
    The Praise on this account fills up and throngs
Eternity brimfull, doth overflow
    The Heavens vast with rich Angelick Songs.
    How should I blush? how Tremble at this thing,
    Not having yet my gamut,[1] learn'd to sing.

But, Lord, as burnish't Sun Beams forth out fly,
    Let Angell-Shine forth in my Life out flame,
That I may grace thy gracefull Family,
    And not to thy Relations be a shame.
    Make mee thy Grafft, be thou my Golden Stock:
    Thy Glory then I'le make my fruits and Crop.

Meditation Thirty

2 CORINTHIANS V: 17: Therefore if any man be in Christ, he is a new creature.

The Daintiest Draught thy Pensill ever[1] Drew:
  The finest vessell, Lord, thy fingers fram'de,
The stateli'st Palace Angells e're did view,
    Under thy Hatch betwixt Decks here Contain'd:
    Broke, marred, spoild, undone, Defil'd, doth ly
    In Rubbish ruinde by thine Enemy.

What Pittie's this? Oh Sunshine Art! What Fall?
  Thou that more Glorious wast than glories Wealth!
More Golden far than Gold! Lord, on whose Wall
    Thy scutchons hung, the Image of thyselfe!
    It's ruinde, and must rue, though Angells should
    To hold it up, heave while their Heart Strings hold.

But yet thou stem of Davids stock, when dry
  And shrivled held, although most green was lopt;
Whose sap a sovereign sodder is, whereby
    The breach repared is in which its dropt.
    Oh Gracious Twig! thou Cut off? bleed rich juyce
    T' Cement the Breach, and Glories shine reduce?

Oh, Lovely One! how doth thy Loveliness
  Beam through the Chrystall Casements of the Eyes
Of Saints and Angells, sparkling Flakes of Fresh
    Heart Ravishing Beauty, filling up their joyes?
    And th' Divells too; if Envies Pupills stood
    Not peeping there these sparkling Rayes t'exclude?

Thou Rod of Davids Root, Branch of his Bough:
  My Lord, repare thy Palace, Deck thy Place.
I'm but a Flesh and Blood bag: Oh! do thou
    Sill, Plate, Ridge, Rib, and Rafter me with Grace.
    Renew my Soule, and guild it all within:
    And hang thy Saving Grace on ery Pin.

My Soule, Lord, make thy Shining Temple, pave
    Its Floore all o're with Orient Grace: thus guild
It o're with Heavens gold: Its Cabbins have
    Thy Treasuries with Choicest thoughts up filld.
    Pourtray thy Glorious Image round about
    Upon thy Temple Walls within and Out.

Garnish thy Hall with Gifts, Lord, from above
    With that Rich Coate of Male, thy Righteousness;
Truth, Belt; the Spirit, Sword; the Buckler, Love;
    Hope's Helmet; and the Shield of Faith kept fresh.
    The Scutchons of thy Honour make my Sign,
    As Garland[1] Tuns are badges made of Wine.

New mould, new make me thus, me new Create,
    Renew in me a spirit right, pure, true.
Lord, make me thy New Creature, then new make
    All things to thy New Creature here anew:
    New Heart, New thoughts, New Words, New wayes likewise,
    New Glory then shall to thyselfe arise.

Meditation Thirty-Three

1 CORINTHIANS III: 22: Whether Paul, or Apollos, or Cephas, or the world, or life, or death, or things present, or things to come; all are your's.

My Lord, my Life,[1] can Envy ever bee
    A Golden Vertue? Then would God I were
Top full thereof untill it colours mee
    With yellow streaks for thy Deare sake most Deare;
    Till I be Envious made by't at myselfe:
    As scarcely loving thee, my Life, my Health.

Oh! what strange Charm encrampt my Heart with spite,
    Making my Love gleame out upon a Toy?
Lay out Cart Loads of Love upon a mite?
    Scarce lay a mite of Love on thee, my Joy?
    Oh! Lovely thou! Shalt not thou loved bee?
    Shall I ashame thee thus? Oh! shame for mee!

Nature's amaz'de. Oh, monstrous thing, Quoth shee,
    Not Love my life? What Violence doth split
True Love and Life, that they should sunder'd bee?
    She doth not lay such Eggs, nor on them sit.
    How do I sever then my Heart with all
    Its Powers whose Love scarce to my Life doth crawle.

Glory lin'de out a Paradise in Power
    Where e'ry seed a Royall Coach became
For Life to ride in, to each shining Flower.
    And made mans Flower with glory all ore flame.
    Hells Inkfac'de Elfe black Venom spat upon
    The same, and kill'd it. So that Life is gone.

Life thus abus'de fled to the golden Arke,
    Lay lockt up there in Mercie's seate inclosde:
Which did incorporate it whence its Sparke
    Enlivens all things in this Arke inclos'de.
    Oh, glorious Arke! Life's Store-House full of Glee!
    Shall not my Love safe lockt up ly in thee?

Lord, arke my Soule safe in thyselfe, whereby
  I and my Life again may joyned bee.
That I may finde what once I did destroy
  Again Confer'de upon my soul in thee.
  Thou art this Golden Ark, this Living Tree,
  Where life lies treasurde up for all in thee.

Oh! Graft me in this Tree of Life within
  The Paradise of God, that I may live.
Thy Life make live in mee; I'le then begin
  To beare thy Living Fruits, and them forth give.
  Give mee my Life this way; and I'le bestow
  My Love on thee, my Life. And it shall grow.

Meditation Thirty-Eight

1 JOHN II: 1: And if any man sin, we have an advocate with the Father.

Oh! What a thing is Man? Lord, Who am I?
    That thou shouldst give him Law (Oh! golden Line)
To regulate his Thoughts, Words, Life thereby:
    And judge him wilt thereby too in thy time.
    A Court of Justice thou in heaven holdst,
    To try his Case while he's here housd on mould.

How do thy Angells lay before thine eye
    My Deeds both White and Black I dayly doe?
How doth thy Court thou Pannellst there them try?
    But flesh complains. What right for this? let's know!
    For right or wrong, I can't appeare unto't.
    And shall a sentence Pass on such a suite?

Soft; blemish not this golden Bench, or place.
    Here is no Bribe, nor Colourings to hide,
Nor Pettifogger to befog the Case;
    But Justice hath her Glory here well tri'de:
    Her spotless Law all spotted Cases tends;
    Without Respect or Disrespect them ends.

God's Judge himselfe, and Christ Atturny is;
    The Holy Ghost Regesterer is founde.
Angells the sergeants are, all Creatures kiss
    The booke, and doe as Evidence abounde.
    All Cases pass according to pure Law,
    And in the sentence is no Fret nor flaw.

What saith, my soule? Here all thy Deeds are tri'de.
    Is Christ thy Advocate to pleade thy Cause?
Art thou his Client? Such shall never slide.
    He never lost his Case: he pleads such Laws
    As Carry do the same, nor doth refuse
    The Vilest sinners Case that doth him Choose.

This is his Honour, not Dishonour: nay,
  No Habeas-Corpus 'gainst his Clients came;
For all their Fines his Purse doth make down pay.
  He Non-Suites Satan's suite or Casts the same.
  He'l plead thy Case, and not accept a Fee.
  He'l plead Sub Forma Pauperis for thee.

My Case is bad. Lord, be my Advocate.
  My sin is red: I'me under Gods Arrest.
Thou hast the Hit of Pleading; plead my state.
  Although it's bad, thy Plea will make it best.
  If thou wilt plead my Case before the King,
  I'le Waggon Loads of Love and Glory bring.

Meditation Forty-Two

REVELATIONS III: 21: To him that overcometh will
I grant to sit with me in my throne.

Apples of gold, in silver pictures shrin'de,
   Enchant the appetite, make mouths to water:
And Loveliness in Lumps, tunn'd and enrin'de[1]
   In Jasper Cask, when tapt, doth briskly vaper:
    Brings forth a birth of Keyes[2] t' unlock Loves Chest,
    That Love, like Birds, may fly to 't from its nest.

Such is my Lord, and more. But what strang[e] thing
   Am I become? Sin rusts my Lock all o're.
Though he ten thousand Keyes all on a string
   Takes out, scarce one is found, unlocks the Doore;
    Which ope, my Love crincht[3] in a Corner lies
    Like some Shrunk Crickling[4]: and scarce can rise.

Lord, ope the Doore: rub off my Rust, Remove
   My sin, And Oyle my Lock: (Dust there doth shelfe).
My Wards will trig before thy Key: my Love
   Then, as enliven'd, leape will on thyselve.
    It needs must be, that giving handes receive
    Again Receivers Hearts, furld in Love Wreath.

Unkey my Heart: unlock thy Wardrobe: bring
   Out royall Robes: adorne my Soule, Lord: so,
My Love in rich attire shall on my King
   Attend, and honour on him well bestow.
    In Glory he prepares for his a place,
    Whom he doth all beglory here with grace.

He takes them to the shining threashould cleare
   Of his bright Palace, cloath'd in Grace's flame.
Then takes them in thereto, not onely there
   To have a Prospect, but possess the same:
    The Crown of Life, the Throne of Glorys Place,
    The Fathers House blancht o're with orient Grace.

Can'an in golden print enwalld with jems:
  A Kingdome rim'd with Glory round: in fine,
A glorious Crown pal'de thick with all the stems
  Of Grace, and of all Properties Divine.
  How happy wilt thou make mee when these shall
  As a bless't Heritage unto mee fall?

Adorn me, Lord, with Holy Huswifry:
  All blanch my Robes with Clusters of thy Graces:
Thus lead me to thy threashold: give mine Eye
  A Peephole there to see bright glories Chases.
  Then take mee in: I'le pay, when I possess
  Thy Throne, to thee the Rent in Happiness.

Meditation Forty-Nine

MATTHEW XXV: 21: Enter thou into the joy of thy lord.

Lord, do away my Motes and Mountains great.
   My nut is vitiate. Its kirnell rots:
Come, kill the Worm that doth its kirnell eate,
   And strike thy sparkes within my tinderbox.
    Drill through my metall heart an hole, wherein
    With graces Cotters to thyselfe it pin.

A Lock of Steel upon my Soule, whose key
   The serpent keeps, I feare, doth lock my doore:
O pick 't: and through the key-hole make thy way,
   And enter in, and let thy joyes run o're.
    My Wards are rusty. Oyle them till they trig
    Before thy golden key: thy Oyle makes glib.

Take out the Splinters of the World that stick
   Do in my heart. Friends, Honours, Riches, and
The Shivers in't of Hell whose venoms quick
   And firy, make it swoln and ranckling stand.
    These wound and kill: those shackle strongly to
    Poore knobs of Clay, my heart: hence sorrows grow.

Cleanse and enlarge my kask: it is too small:
   And tartariz'd with worldly dregs dri'de in 't.
It's bad mouth'd too: and though thy joyes do Call
   That boundless are, it ever doth them stint.
    Make me thy Chrystall Caske: those wines in't tun
    That in the Rivers of thy joyes do run.

Lord, make me, though suck't through a straw or Quill,
   Tast of the Rivers of thy joyes, some drop.
'Twill sweeten me: and all my Love distill
   Into thy glass; and me for joy make hop.
    'Twill turn my water into wine, and fill
    My Harp with Songs my Masters joyes distill.

Meditation Three

ROMANS V: 14: [Adam:] who is the figure of him that was
to come.

Like to the Marigold, I blushing close
  My golden blossoms when thy sun goes down:
Moist'ning my leaves with Dewy Sighs, half frose
  By the nocturnall Cold, that hoares my Crown.
    Mine Apples ashes[1] are in apple shells,
    And dirty too: strange and bewitching spells!

When, Lord, mine Eye doth spie thy Grace to beame
  Thy Mediatoriall glory in the shine,
Out spouted so from Adams typick streame,
  And Emblemiz'd in Noahs pollisht shrine:
    Thine theirs outshines so far it makes their glory
    In brightest Colours, seem a smoaky story.

But when mine Eye full of these beams doth cast
  Its rayes upon my dusty essence thin,
Impregnate with a Sparke Divine defac'de,
  All candi[e]d o're with Leprosie of Sin,
    Such Influences on my Spirits light,
    Which them as bitter gall, or Cold ice smite.

My brissled sins hence do so horrid peare,
  None but thyselfe, (and thou deck't up must bee
In thy Transcendent glory sparkling cleare)
  A Mediator unto God for mee.
    So high they rise, Faith scarce can toss a Sight
    Over their head upon thyselfe to light.

Is't possible such glory, Lord, ere should
  Center its Love on me, Sins Dunghill else?
My Case up take? make it its own? Who would
  Wash with his blood my blots out? Crown his shelfe,

Or Dress his golden Cupboard with such ware?
This makes my pale facde hope almost despare.

Yet let my Titimouses[1] Quill suck in
   Thy Graces milk Pails some small drop: or Cart
A Bit or Splinter of some Ray, the wing
   Of Grace's sun sprindg'd out, into my heart:
   To build there Wonders Chappell where thy Praise
   Shall be the Psalms sung forth in gracious layes.

Meditation Seven

PSALMS CV: 17: He sent a man before them, even Joseph,
who was sold for a servant.

All Dull, my Lord, my Spirits, flat and dead;
    All water sockt and sapless to the skin.
Oh! Screw mee up, and make my Spirits bed
    Thy quickening vertue, for my inke is dim;
      My pensill blunt. Doth Joseph type out thee?
      Haraulds of Angells sing out, Bow the Knee.

Is Josephs glorious shine a Type of thee?
    How bright art thou? He envi'de was as well.
And so wast thou. He's stript and pick't, poore hee,
    Into the pit. And so was thou. They shell
      Thee of thy kirnell. He by Judah's sold
      For twenty bits: thirty for thee [we're][1] told.

Joseph was tempted by his Mistress vile;
    Thou by the Divell, but both shame the foe.
Joseph was cast into the jayle awhile,
    And so was thou. Sweet apples mellow so.
      Joseph did from his jayle to glory run:
      Thou from Death's pallot rose like morning sun.

Joseph layes in against the Famine, and
    Thou dost prepare the Bread of Life for thine;
He bought with Corn for Pharaoh men and Land;
    Thou with thy Bread mak'st such themselves Consign
      Over to thee, that eate it. Joseph makes
      His brethren bow before him. Thine too quake.

Joseph constrains his Brethren till their sins
    Do gall their Souls. Repentance babbles fresh.
Thou treatest sinners till Repentance springs.
    Then with him sendst a Benjamin-like messe.

Joseph doth Cheare his humble brethren. Thou
Dost stud with joy the mourning Saints that bow.

Josephs bright shine th' Eleven Tribes must preach,
    And thine Apostles now Eleven, thine.
They beare his presents to his Friends: thine reach
    Thine unto thine thus now behold a shine.
    How hast thou pensild out, my Lord, most bright,
    Thy glorious Image here on Josephs Light.

This I bewaile, in me under this shine,
    To see so dull a Colour in my Skin.
Lord, lay thy brightsome Colours on me: thine;
    Scoure thou my pipes, then play thy tunes therein.
    I will not hang my Harp in Willows by,
    While thy sweet praise, my Tunes doth glorify.

Meditation Eleven

JUDGES XIII: 3: And the angel of the Lord appeared unto the woman.

Eternall Love, burnisht in Glory thick,
   Doth but[t] and Center in thee, Lord, my joy.
Thou portrai'd art in Colours bright, that stick
   Their Glory on the Choicest Saints, whereby
   They are thy Pictures made. Samson exceld
   Herein thy Type, as he thy foes once queld.

An Angell tells his mother of his birth.
   An Angell telleth thine of thine. Ye two
Both Males that ope the Womb in Wedlock Kerfe;[1]
   Both Nazarited from the Womb up grow.
   He after pitchy night a Sunshine grows,
   And thou the Sun of Righteousness up rose.

His Love did Court a Gentile spouse; and thine
   Espous'd a Gentile to bebride thyselfe.
His Gentile Bride apostatizd betime:
   Apostasy in thine grew full of Wealth.
   He sindgd the Authours of 't with Foxes tails;
   And foxy men by thee on thine prevaile.

The Fret now rose. Thousands upon him pour.
   An asses Jaw his javling is, whereby
He slew a Thousand, heap by heap that hour.
   Thou by weak means mak'st many thousands fly.
   Thou ribbon-like wast platted in his Locks,
   And hence he thus his Enemies did box.

He's by his Friend betray'd, for money sold,
   Took, bound, blindfolded, made a May game Flout;
Dies freely with great sinners, when they hold
   A Sacred Feast: with arms stretcht greatly out:

Slew more by death, than in his Life he slew.
And all such things, my Lord, in thee are true.

Samson at Gaza went to bed to sleep.
    The Gazites watch him, and the Soldiers thee.
He Champion stout at midnight rose full deep,
    Took Gaza's Gate on's back: away went hee.
    Thou rose didst from thy Grave, and also tookst
    Deaths Doore away, throwing it off o' th' hooks.

Thus all the shine that Samson wore is thine,
    Thine in the Type. Oh, Glorious One, Rich glee!
Gods Love hath made thee thus. Hence thy bright shine
    Commands our Love to bow thereto the Knee.
    Thy Glory chargeth us in Sacrifice
    To make our Hearts and Love to thee to rise.

But woe is me! my heart doth run out to
    Poor bits of Clay, or dirty Gayes[1] embrace:
Doth leave thy Lovely Selfe for loveless shows;
    For lumps of Lust, nay, sorrow and disgrace.
    Alas, poore Soule! a Pardon, Lord, I crave.
    I have dishonourd thee and all I have.

Be thou my Samson, Lord, a Rising Sun
    Of Righteousness unto my Soule, I pray.
Conquour my Foes. Let Graces Spouts all run
    Upon my Soule, o're which thy sunshine lay.
    And set me in thy Sunshine, make each flower
    Of Grace in me, thy Praise perfum'd out poure.

Meditation Eighteen

SECOND SERIES

HEBREWS XIII: 10: We have an altar . . .

A Bran, a Chaff, a very Barly yawn,[1]
   An Husk, a Shell, a Nothing, nay, yet worse:
A Thistle, Bryer prickle, pricking Thorn,
   A Lump of Lewdeness, Pouch of Sin, a purse
   Of Naughtiness I am, yea, what not, Lord?
   And wilt thou be mine Altar? and my Lord?

Mine Heart's a Park or Chase of sins: Mine Head
   'S a Bowling Alley: sins play Ninehole here.
Phansy's a Green: sin Barly-breaks[2] in't led.
   Judgment's a pingle:[3] Blindeman's Buff's plaid there.
   Sin playes at Coursey-Park[4] within my Minde;
   My Will's a Walke in which it aires what's blinde.

Sure then I lack Atonement. Lord, me help.
   Thy Shittim Wood[5] o'relaid with wealthy brass
Was an Atoning altar, and sweet smelt:
   But if orelaid with pure pure gold it was,
   It was an Incense Altar, all perfum'd
   With Odours, wherein, Lord, thou thus was bloom'd.

Did this ere during Wood, when thus orespread
   With these erelasting Metalls altarwise,
Type thy Eternall Plank of Godhead, wed
   Unto our Mortall Chip, its sacrifice?
   Thy Deity mine Altar; Manhood thine.
   Mine Offring on't for all men's sins, and mine?

This Golden Altar puts such weight into
   The sacrifices offer'd on't, that it
Ore weighs the Weight of all the sins that flow
   In thine Elect. This Wedge and beetle split

The knotty Logs of Vengeance too to shivers,
And from their Guilt and shame, them cleare delivers.

This Holy Altar by its Heavenly fire
    Refines our Offerings; casts out their dross,
And sanctifies their Gold by its rich 'tire;
        And all their steams with Holy Odours boss.
        Pillars of Frankincense and rich Perfume
        They 'tone Gods nosthrills with, off from this Loom.

Good News, Good Sirs, more good than comes within
    The Canopy of Angells; Heavens Hall
Allows no better: this atones for sin.
        My Glorious God, whose Grace here thickest falls,
        May I my Barly yawn, Bran, Bryer Claw,
        Lay on't a Sacrifice? or Chaff or Straw?

Shall I my sin Pouch lay, on thy Gold Bench,
    My Offering, Lord, to thee? I've such alone,
But have no better; for my sins do drench
        My very best unto their very bone.
        And shall mine offering by thine Altars fire
        Refin'd and sanctifi'd, to God aspire?

Amen: ev'n so be it. I now will climb
    The stares up to thine Altar, and on't lay
Myselfe, and services, even for its shrine.
        My sacrifice brought thee, accept I pray.
        My Morn and Evning Offerings I'le bring,
        And on this Golden Altar Incense fling.

Lord, let thy Deity mine Altar bee,
    And make thy Manhood, on't my sacrifice
For mine Atonement. Make them both for mee.
        My Altar t'sanctify my gifts likewise,
        That so myselfe and service on't may bring
        Its worth along with them to thee my king.

The thoughts whereof, do make my tunes as fume,
  From off this Altar rise to thee Most High.
And all their steams stufft with thy Altars bloome,
  My Sacrifice of Praise in Melody.
  Let thy bright Angells catch my tune, and sing 't,
  That Equalls Davids Michtam[1] which is in 't.

Meditation Thirty

MATTHEW XII: 40: For as Jonas was three days and three nights in the whale's belly; so shall the Son of man be three days and three nights in the heart of the earth.

Prest down with sorrow, Lord, not for my Sin,
 But with Saint 'Tonys Cross¹ I crossed groane.
Thus my leane Muses garden thwarts the spring:
 Instead of Anthems, breatheth her a hone.²
 But duty raps upon her doore for verse,
 That makes her bleed a poem through her searce.³

When, Lord, man was a mir[r]or of thy Works
 In happy state, adorn'd with Glory's Wealth,
What heedless thing was hee? The serpent lurks
 Under an apple paring, and by stealth
 Destroy'd her Glory. O poor keeper hee
 Was of himselfe: lost God, and lost his Glee.

Christ, as a Turtle Dove, puts out his Wing.
 Lay all on mee; I will, saith hee, Convay
Away thy fault, and answer for thy sin.
 Thou'st be the Stewhouse⁴ of my Grace, and lay
 It and thyselfe out in my service pure,
 And I will for thy sake the storm Endure.

Jonas did type this thing, who ran away
 From God and, shipt for Tarsus, fell asleep.
A storm lies on the Ship: the Seamen they
 Bestir their stumps, and at wits end do weep:
 'Wake, Jonas:' who saith, 'Heave me over deck;
 The Storm will Cease then; all lies on my neck.'

They cast him overboard out of the ship.
 The tempest terrible lies thereby still.
A Mighty Whale nam'd Neptunes Dog⁵ doth skip

At such a Boon, whose greedy gorge can't kill,
Neither Concoct this gudgeon, but its Chest
Became the Prophets Coffin for the best.

He three dayes here lies trancifi'de[1] and prayes,
  Prooves working Physick in the fishes Crop:
Maybe in th' Euxine, or the Issick Bay[2]
  She puking falls, and he alive out drops.
  She vomits him alive out on the Land,
  Whence he to Ninive receives command.

A sermon he unto the Gentiles preach't,
  'Yet fortie dayes, and Nin've is destroy'd!'
Space granted, this Repentance doth them teach:
  God pardons them, and thus they ruine 'void.
  Oh! Sweet, Sweet Providence, rich Grace hath splic'te
  This Overture to be a type of Christ.

Jonas our Turtle Dove, I Christ intend,
  Is in the ship for Tarsus under saile.
A fiery storm tempestiously doth spend
  The Vessill and its hands: all Spirits faile;
  The ship will sink, or wrack upon the rocks,
  Unless the tempest cease the same to box.

None can it Charm but Jonas. Christ up posts,
  Is heaved overboard into the sea:
The Dove must die, the storm gives up its Ghost,
  And Neptune's Dogg leapes at him as a Prey,
  Whose stomach is his Grave where he doth sleep
  Three Dayes sepulchred, Jonas in the Deep.

The Grave him swallow'd down as a rich Pill
  Of Working Physick full of Virtue, which
Doth purge Death's Constitution of its ill,
  And womble-Crops[3] her stomach where it sticks.
  It heaves her stomach till her hasps off fly:
  And out hee comes cast up, rais'd up thereby.

In glorious Grace he to the Heathen goes,
   Envites them to Repentance. They accept.
Oh! Happy Message squandering Curst foes:
   Grace in her glorious Charriot here rides decks.
   Wrath's Fire is quencht: and Graces sun out shines;
   Death on her deathbed lies, Consumes and pines.

Here is my rich Atonement in thy Death;
   My Lord, nought is so sweet, though sweat it cost.
This turns from me Gods wrath: thy sweet sweet breath
   Revives my heart: thy Rising up, o're bosst
   My Soule with Hope, seeing acquittance in't:
   That all my sins are kill'd, that did mee sinke.

I thanke thee, Lord, thy death hath dead'ned quite
   The Dreadfull Tempest. Let thy Dovy wings
Oreshadow me, and all my Faults benight,
   And with Celestiall Dews my soule besprindge.[1]
   In angells Quires I'le then my Michtams[2] sing,
   Upon my Jonah Elem Rechokim.[3]

Meditation Thirty-Three

SECOND SERIES

JOHN XV: 13: Greater love hath no man than this, that a man lay down his life for his friends.

Walking, my Lord, within thy Paradise,[1]
   I finde a Fruite, whose Beauty smites mine Eye,
And Taste my Tooth, that had no Core nor Vice:
    An Hony Sweet, that's never rotting, ly
    Under a Tree, which view'd, I knew to bee
    The Tree of Life, whose bulk's Theanthropie.[2]

And looking up, I saw its boughs all bow
   With Clusters of this Fruit that it doth bring,
Nam'de Greatest LOVE, and well. For bulk and brow
    Thereof, of th' sap of Godhood-Manhood spring.
    What Love is here for kinde? What sort? How much?
    None ever, but the Tree of Life, bore such.

Who is the Object of this Love? and in
   Whose mouth doth fall the Apple of this tree?
Is Man? A Sinner? Such a Wormhole thing?
    Oh! matchless Love, laid out on such as Hee!
    Should Gold wed Dung, should Stars wooe Lobster Claws,
    It would no wonder, like this Wonder, cause.

Is sinfull Man the object of this Love?
   What then doth it for this its Object doe?
It doth require a purging far above
    The whiteness Sope and Nitre can bestow:
    (Else Justice will its Object take away,
    Out of its bosome, and to hell 't convay.)

Hence in it steps; to justice saith, I'll make
   Thee satisfaction, and my Object shine.
I'l slay my humane Nature for thy sake,
    Fil[l']d with the Worthiness of thy Divine.

Make pay therewith. The Fruite doth sacrifice
The tree that bore 't. This for its object dies.

An Higher round upon this golden scale
Love cannot Climbe, than to lay down the Life
Of him that loves, for him belov'd to bail;
Thereby to satisfy, and end all strife.
Thou lay'st, my Lord, thy life down for thy Friend,
And greater Love than this none can out send.

Then make me, Lord, thy Friend, I humbly pray,
Though I thereby should be deare bought by thee:
Not dearer yet than others, for the pay
Is but the same for others as for mee.
If I be in thy booke, my Life shall proove
My Love to thee; an Offering to thy Love.

Meditation Fifty-Six

JOHN XV: 24: If I had not done among them the works
which none other man did, they had not had sin: but
now have they both seen and hated both me and my
Father.

Should I with silver tooles delve through the Hill
    Of Cordilera[1] for rich thoughts, that I
My Lord, might weave with an angelick skill
      A Damask Web of Velvet Verse, thereby
      To deck thy Works up, all my Web would run
      To rags and jags: so snick-snarld to the thrum.

Thine are so rich: within, without refin'd:
    No worke like thine. No Fruits so sweete that grow
On th' trees of righteousness of Angell kinde,
      And Saints, whose limbs reev'd[2] with them bow down low.
      Should I search ore the Nutmeg Gardens shine,
      Its fruits in flourish are but skegs[3] to thine.

The Clove, when in its White-green'd blossoms shoots,[4]
    Some Call the pleasantst s[c]ent the World doth show,
None Eye e're saw, nor nose e're smelt such Fruits,
      My Lord, as thine, Thou Tree of Life in 'ts blow.
      Thou Rose of Sharon, Vallies Lilly true,
      Thy Fruits most sweet and glorious ever grew.

Thou art a Tree of Perfect nature trim,
    Whose golden lining is of perfect Grace,
Perfum'de with Deity unto the brim,
      Whose fruits, of the perfection, grow, of Grace.
      Thy Buds, thy Blossoms, and thy fruits adorne
      Thyselfe and Works, more shining than the morn.

Art, natures Ape, hath many brave things done:[5]
    As th' Pyramids, the Lake of Meris vast,
The Pensile Orchards built in Babylon,

Psammitich's Labyrinth, (arts Cramping task)
Archimedes his Engins made for war,
Romes Golden House, Titus his Theater.

The Clock of Strasburgh, Dresdens Table-sight,
  Regsamonts Fly of Steele about that flew,
Turrian's Wooden Sparrows in a flight,
  And th' Artificiall man Aquinas slew,
    Mark Scaliota's Lock and Key and Chain
    Drawn by a Flea, in our Queen Betties reign.

Might but my pen in natures Inventory
  Its progress make, 't might make such things to jump,
All which are but Inventions Vents or glory:
  Wits Wantonings, and Fancies frollicks plump:
    Within whose maws lies buried Times, and Treasures,
    Embalmed up in thick dawbd sinfull pleasures.

Nature doth better work than Art, yet thine
  Out vie both works of nature and of Art.
Natures Perfection and the perfect shine
  Of Grace attend thy deed in ev'ry part.
    A Thought, a Word, and Worke of thine, will kill
    Sin, Satan, and the Curse: and Law fulfill.

Thou art the Tree of Life in Paradise,
  Whose lively branches are with Clusters hung
Of Lovely fruits, and Flowers more sweet than spice.
  Bende down to us, and doe outshine the sun.
    Delightfull unto God, doe man rejoyce
    The pleasant'st fruits in all Gods Paradise.

Lord, feed mine eyes then with thy Doings rare,
  And fat my heart with these ripe fruites thou bear'st;
Adorn my Life well with thy works; make faire
  My Person with apparrell thou prepar'st.
    My Boughs shall loaded bee with fruits that spring
    Up from thy Works, while to thy praise I sing.

Meditation Sixty

SECOND SERIES

1 CORINTHIANS X: 4: And did all drink the same spiritual drink.

Ye Angells bright, pluck from your Wings a Quill;
    Make me a pen thereof that best will write:
Lende me your fancy and Angellick skill
    To treate this Theme, more rich than Rubies bright.
    My muddy Inke and Cloudy fancy dark
    Will dull its glory, lacking highest Art.

An Eye at Centre righter may describe
    The Worlds Circumferentiall glory vast,
As in its nutshell bed it snugs fast ti'de,
    Than any angells pen can glory Cast
    Upon this Drink drawn from the Rock, tapt by
    The Rod of God, in Horeb, typickly.

Sea water strain'd through Minerall, Rocks, and Sands,
    Well Clarifi'de by Sunbeams, Dulcifi'de,
Insipid, Sordid, Swill, Dishwater stands.
    But here's a Rock of Aqua-Vitae tri'de!
    When once God broacht it, out a River came
    To bath and bibble in, for Israels train.

Some rocks have sweat. Some Pillar[s] bled out tears,
    But here's a River in a Rock up tun[n]'d,
Not of Sea Water nor of Swill. It's beere!
    No Nectar like it! Yet it once unbun[g]d,
    A River down out runs through ages all,
    A Fountain opte, to wash off Sin and Fall.

Christ is this Horebs Rock, the streames that slide
    A River is of Aqua Vitae Deare,
Yet costs us nothing, gushing from his side:
    Celestiall Wine our sinsunk souls to cleare.
    This Rock and Water, Sacramentall Cup
    Are made, Lords Supper Wine for us to sup.

This Rock's the Grape that Zions Vineyard bore,
    Which Moses Rod did smiting pound, and press,
Untill its blood, the brooke of Life, run ore:
    All Glorious Grace, and Gracious Righteousness.
    We in this brook must bath: and with faiths quill
    Suck Grace and Life out of this Rock our fill.

Lord, oynt me with this Petro oyle: I'm sick.
    Make mee drinke Water of the Rock: I'm dry.
Me in this fountain wash: my filth is thick.
    I'm faint: give Aqua Vitae or I dy.
    If in this stream thou cleanse and Chearish mee,
    My Heart thy Hallelujahs Pipe shall bee.

Meditation Sixty-Two

SECOND SERIES

CANTICLES I: 12: While the king sitteth at his table, my spike-
nard sendeth forth the smell thereof.

Oh! thou, my Lord, thou king of Saints, here mak'st
    A royall Banquet, thine to entertain
With rich and royall fare, Celestiall Cates,
      And sittest at the Table rich of fame.
      Am I bid to this Feast? Sure Angells stare,
      Such Rugged looks, and Ragged robes I ware.

I'le surely come; Lord, fit mee for this feast:
    Purge me with Palma Christi from my sin.[1]
With Plastrum Gratiae Dei, or at least
      Unguent Apostolorum healing bring.
      Give me thy Sage and Savory: me dub
      With Golden Rod, and with Saint Johns Wort good.

Root up my Henbain, Fawnbain, Divells bit,
    My Dragons, Chokewort, Crosswort, Ragwort, vice:
And set my knot with Honysuckles, stick
      Rich Herb-a-Grace, and Grains of Paradise,
      Angelica, yea, Sharons Rose the best,
      And Herba Trinitatis in my breast.

Then let thy Sweetspike sweat its liquid Dew
    Into my Crystall Viall, and there swim.
And, as thou at thy Table in Rich Shew
      With royal Dainties, sweet discourse as King
      Dost Welcome thine, My Spiknard with its smell
      Shall vapour out perfumed Spirits Well.

Whether I at thy Table Guest do sit,
    And feed my tast, or Wait, and fat mine Eye
And Eare with Sights and Sounds, Heart Raptures fit:
      My Spicknard breaths its sweet perfumes with joy.
      My heart thy Viall with this spicknard fill,
      Perfumed praise to thee then breath it will.

Meditation Seventy-Six

PHILIPPIANS III: 21: Who shall change our vile
body, that it may be fashioned like unto his glori-
ous body . . .

Will yee be neighbourly, ye Angells bright?
  Then lend mee your Admiring Facultie:
Wonders presented stand, above my might,
  That call from mee the highest Extasie.
  If you deny mee this, my pimping Soule,
  These Wonders pins up in an Auger hole.

If my Rush Candle on its wick-ware flame
  Of Ignis lambens,[1] Oh! bright garb indeed:
What then, when Flakes of flaming Glory train
  From thy bright glorious bulk to 'ray my weed.
  What, my vile Body like thy Glorious, Form'd?
  What Wonder here? My body thus adorn'd!

What, shall mine hempen harle move in thy Loome
  Into a web (an harden[2] web indeed),
Be made its Makers Tent Cloth,[3] I presume.
  Within these Curtains Grace keeps hall, and breeds:
  But shall my harden-hangings ever ware
  A bright bright glory like thy body faire?

Meethinks thy smile doth make thy Footstoole so
  Spread its green carpet 'fore thy feet for joy,
And Bryers climb thereup, bright roses blow
  Out in sweet reechs to meet thee in the sky:
  And makes the sportive starrs play Hide-and-Seek,
  And on thy bodies Glory peeping keep.

And shall not I (whose form transformd shall be,
  To be shap'te like thy glorious body, Lord,
That Angells bright, as gaster'd,[4] gaze at mee

To see such Glory on my dresser board),
Transported be hereat for very joy,
Whose intrest lies herein, and gloriously?

What, shall the frosty Rhime upon my locks
   Congeale my braine with Chilly dews, whereby
My Phansie is benumbd: and put in stocks,
   And thaws not into steams of reeching joy?
   Oh! strange Ingratitude! Let not this Frame
   Abide, Lord, in mee. Fire mee with thy flame.

Lord, let thy Glorious Body send such rayes
   Into my Soule, as ravish shall my heart,
That Thoughts how thy Bright Glory out shall blaze
   Upon my body, may such Rayes thee dart.
   My Tunes shall dance then on these Rayes, and Caper
   Unto thy Praise: when Glory lights my Taper.

Meditation Seventy-Seven

ZECHARIAH IX: 11: As for thee also, by the blood of thy
covenant I have sent forth thy prisoners out of the pit
wherein is no water.

A State, a State, Oh! Dungeon State indeed,
   In which mee headlong, long agoe Sin pitcht:
As dark as Pitch; where Nastiness doth breed:
   And Filth defiles: and I am with it ditcht.
   A Sinfull State: This Pit no Water's in't.
   A Bugbare State: as black as any inke.

I once at Singing on the Summit high
   'Mong the Celestiall Coire in Musick Sweet:
On highest bough of Paradisall joy;
   Glory and Innocence did in mee meet.
   I as a Gold-Fincht Nighting Gale, tun'd ore
   Melodious Songs 'fore Glorie's Palace Doore.

But on this bough I tuning Pearcht not long:
   Th'Infernall Foe shot out a Shaft from Hell;
A Fiery Dart pilde with Sins poison Strong:
   That Struck my heart, and down I headlong fell:
   And from the Highest Pinicle of Light
   Into this Lowest pit more darke than night.

A Pit indeed of Sin: No water's here:
   Whose bottom's furthest off from Heaven bright.
And is next doore to Hell Gate: to it neer:
   And here I dwell in Sad and Solemn night.
   My Gold-Fincht Angell Feathers dapled in
   Hells Scarlet Dy fat, blood red grown with Sin.

I in this Pit all Destitute of Light
   Cram'd full of Horrid Darkness, here do Crawle
Up over head, and Eares, in Nauseous plight:
   And Swinelike Wallow in this mire and Gall:

No Heavenly Dews nor Holy Waters drill:
Nor Sweet Aire Brieze, nor Comfort here distill.

Here for Companions, are Fears, Heart-Achs, Grief,
    Frogs, Toads, Newts, Bats, Horrid Hob-Goblins, Ghosts,
Ill Spirits haunt this Pit: and no reliefe:
    Nor Coard can fetch me hence in Creatures Coasts.
    I who once lodgd at Heavens Palace Gate
    With full Fledgd Angells, now possess this fate.

But yet, my Lord, thy golden Chain of Grace
    Thou canst let down, and draw mee up into
Thy Holy Aire, and Glory's Happy Place,
    Out from these Hellish damps and pit so low.
    And if thy Grace shall do't, My Harp I'le raise,
    Whose Strings toucht by this Grace, Will twang thy praise.

Meditation Eighty-Two

SECOND SERIES

JOHN VI: 53: Except ye eat the flesh of the Son of man, and drink his blood, ye have no life in you.

My tatter'd Fancy; and my Ragged Rymes
   Teem leaden Metaphors: which yet might Serve
To hum a little touching terrene[1] Shines.
   But Spirituall Life doth better fare deserve.
   This thought on, sets my heart upon the Rack:
   I fain would have this Life but han't its knack.

Reason stands for it, moving to persue't,
   But Flesh and Blood are Elementall things
That sink me down, dulling my Spirits fruit.
   Life Animall a Spirituall Sparke ne'er Springs.
   But if thy Altars Coale Enfire my heart,
   With this Blesst Life my Soule will be thy Sparke.

I'm Common matter: Lord thine Altar make mee,
   Then Sanctify thine Altar with thy blood:
I'l offer on't my heart to thee. (Oh! take mee)
   And let thy fire Calcine mine Altars Wood
   Then let thy Spirits breath, (as Bellows) blow,
   That this new kindled Life may flame and glow.

Some Life with Spoon, or Trencher do mentain
   Or Suck its food through a Small Quill or Straw:
But make me, Lord, this Life thou givst, Sustain
   With thy Sweet Flesh and Blood, by Gospell Law.
   Feed it on Zions Pasty Plate-Delights:
   I'de suck it from her Candlesticks Sweet Pipes.

Need makes the Oldwife trot:[2] Necessity
   Saith, I must eate this Flesh, and drinke this blood
If not, no Life's in mee that's worth a Fly;
   This mortall Life, while here, eats mortall Foode

174

That sends out influences to mentaine,
A little while, and then holds back the same.

But Soule Sweet Bread is in Gods Backhouse made
   On Heavens high Dresser Boarde and throughly bakd:
On Zions Gridiron, sapt in'ts dripping trade,
   That all do live that on it do partake,
   Its Flesh and Blood even of the Deity;
   None that do eat and Drinke it, ever dy.

Have I a vitall Sparke even of this Fire?
   How Dull am I? Lord let thy Spirit blow
Upon my Coale, untill its heart is higher,
   And I be quicknd by the same, and Glow.
   Here's Manna, Angell food, to fatten them,
   That I must eate or be a wither'd stem.

Lord, make my Faith thy golden Quill wherethrough
   I vitall Spirits from thy blood may suck.
Make Faith my Grinders, thy Choice Flesh to chew,
   My Witherd Stock shall with frim[1] Fruits be Stuck.
   My Soule shall then in Lively Notes forth ring
   Upon her Virginalls, praise for this thing.

Meditation One Hundred and Ten

MATTHEW XXVI: 30: And when they had sung an hymn, they
went out into the mount of Olives.

The Angells sung a Carole at thy Birth,
   My Lord, and thou thyselfe didst sweetly sing
An Epinicioum[1] at thy Death on Earth.
    And order'st thine, in memory of this thing,
    Thy Holy Supper, closing it at last
     Up with an Hymn, and Choakst the foe thou hast.

This Feast thou madst in memory of thy death:
   Which is disht up most graciously: and towers
Of reeching vapours from thy Grave (Sweet breath)
    Aromatize the Skies: That sweetest Showers,
    Richly perfumed by the Holy Ghost,
     Are rained thence upon the Churches Coast.

Thy Grave beares flowers to dress thy Church withall,
   In which thou dost thy Table dress for thine.
With Gospell Carpet, Chargers, Festivall
    And Spirituall Venison, White Bread and Wine:
    Being the Fruits thy Grave brings forth and hands
     Upon thy Table where thou waiting standst.

Dainties most rich, all spiced o're with Grace,
   That grow out of thy Grave do deck thy Table.
To entertain thy Guests, thou callst, and place
    Allowst, with welcome: (and this is no Fable).
    And with these Guests I am invited to' t,
     And this rich banquet makes me thus a Poet.

Thy Cross planted within thy Coffin beares
   Sweet Blossoms and rich Fruits, whose steams do rise
Out of thy Sepulcher and purge the aire
    Of all Sins damps and fogs that Choake the Skies.

This Fume perfumes Saints hearts as it out peeps,
   Ascending up to bury thee in th' reechs.

Joy stands on tiptoes[1] all the while thy Guests
   Sit at thy Table, ready forth to sing
Its Hallilujahs in sweet musicks dress,
   Waiting for Organs to imploy herein.
   Here matter is allowd to all, rich, high,
   My Lord, to tune thee Hymns melodiously.

Oh! make my heart thy Pipe: the Holy Ghost
   The Breath that fills the same and Spiritually.
Then play on mee, thy pipe, that is almost
   Worn out with piping tunes of Vanity.
   Winde musick is the best, if thou delight
   To play the same thyselfe, upon my pipe.

Hence make me, Lord, thy Golden Trumpet Choice,
   And trumpet thou thyselfe upon the same
Thy heart enravishing Hymns with Sweetest Voice.
   When thou thy Trumpet soundst, thy tunes will flame.
   My heart shall then sing forth thy praises sweet,
   When sounded thus with thy Sepulcher reech.

Make too my Soul thy Cittern, and its wyers
   Make my affections: and rub off their rust
With thy bright Grace: and screw my Strings up higher,
   And tune the same to tunes thy praise most Just.
   Ile close thy Supper then with Hymns most sweet,
   Burr'ing thy Grave in thy Sepulcher's reech.

Meditation One Hundred and Twelve

2 CORINTHIANS V: 14: For the love of Christ constraineth us; because we thus judge, that if one died for all, then were all dead.

Oh! Good, Good, Good, my Lord. What, more Love yet!
　Thou dy for mee! What, am I dead in thee:
What, did Deaths arrow shot at me thee hit?
　Didst slip between that flying shaft and mee?
　Didst make thyselfe Deaths marke shot at for mee?
　So that her Shaft shall fly no far than thee?

Didst dy for mee indeed, and in thy Death
　Take in thy Dying thus my death the Cause.
And lay I dying in thy Dying breath,
　According unto Graces Redemption Laws?
　If one did dy for all, it needs must bee
　That all did dy in one, and from death free.

Infinities fierce firy arrow red
　Shot from the splendid Bow of Justice bright
Did smite thee down, for thine. Thou art their head.
　They di'de in thee. Their death did on thee light.
　They di'de their Death in thee; thy Death is theirs;
　Hence thine is mine; thy death my trespass cleares.·

How sweet is this: my Death lies buried
　Within thy Grave, my Lord, deep under ground.
It is unskin'd, as Carrion rotten Dead.
　For Grace's hand gave Death its deadly wound.
　Deaths no such terrour in th'Saints blesst Coast,
　Its but a harmless Shade: No walking Ghost.

The Painter lies: the Bellfrey Pillars weare
　A false Effigies now of Death alas.
With empty Eyeholes, Butter teeth, bones bare

And spraggling[1] arms, having an Hour Glass
In one grim paw. Th'other a Spade doth hold,
To shew deaths frightfull region under mould.

Whereas its Sting is gone: its life is lost.
    Though unto Christless ones it is most Grim,
Its but a Shade to Saints whose path it Crosst:
    Or Shell or Washen face, in which she sing
    Their Bodies in her lap a Lollaboy
    And sends their Souls to sing their Masters joy.

Lord, let me finde Sin, Curse, and Death that doe
    Belong to me by [thee] slain in thy Grave.
And let thy law my clearing hence bestow,
    And from these things let me acquittance have.
    The Law suffic'de: and I discharg'd, Hence Sing
    Thy praise I will, over Deaths Death and Sin.

GLOSSARY

The following definitions are intended as a guide to the meaning of terms as they were expounded in covenant theology, and as they are found in Taylor's poetry. The definitions follow in particular the exposition of doctrine as set forth in Samuel Willard, *A Compleat Body of Divinity* (Boston, 1726). Standard works, such as the *New English Dictionary* and the *Dictionary of Religion and Ethics* help gloss the wider meaning of terms.

APOSTASY. Though the term essentially implies total abandonment of what one has religiously professed, *(i.e.,* faith in Christ as opposed to mere heresy or schism), it meant for the Puritans the rebellion of man against God's decrees, and his consequent fall and ruin: opposed to Recovery.

ASSURANCE. Individual assurance of salvation, for the seventeenth-century Puritan of New England, was only by way of the Covenant. It is the preliminary step to regeneration; without it no start can be made.

ATTRIBUTES. God possesses two especially important attributes, by which He intends principally to exalt His reasonable creatures: Mercy and Justice. These are His moral perfections. His power as Creator is another attribute; *see* Properties.

BOOK OF NATURE. The works of God as witnessed in the universe about us.

CIVIL RIGHTEOUSNESS. The state wherein man was assumed naturally good or virtuous, but unregenerate; good as a citizen, but not as a saint; *also* called Civility.

COVENANT. Covenant theology was the foundation of Puritanism in New England. The Covenant of Grace, which was its special feature, was first popularized by the English theologian William Perkins, in the 1590's, and developed chiefly by William Ames and John Preston in the early seventeenth century. Covenant theology postulated a compact or agreement between God and Adam, the "federal" head of the race, (hence giving to the doctrine the name sometimes of Federal theology). God freely promised Adam, who in his original state was neither happy nor miserable, eternal happiness to himself and all mankind, his posterity, on condition only that he obey God's injunction. This part of the doctrine is known as the Covenant of Works, since it required of man an active, not a passive, obedience. But by Adam's fall all mankind forfeited the covenant, and hence was subject to eternal damnation. Nevertheless, God, of his sovereign, arbitrary, and gracious free will, instituted a new covenant, called the Covenant of Grace, (the element stressed by Perkins and Ames, and followed in New England), by which mankind was promised hope of eternal life, providing only that he believe in Christ: have faith that God's only begotten son, after crucifixion and death, whereby He "satisfied" the Covenant of Works, ascended to Heaven as intercessor for erring man.

The Puritans, in their exposition of this doctrine, stressed the idea that God's entering into the covenant was voluntary and designed for man's happiness; that after man forfeited salvation by breaking the terms of the first covenant, God's sealing of a new one was unparalleled kindness; that throughout God had treated man as a reasonable creature, not one from whom mere blind obedience was demanded. God had acted with complete justice, but He had willingly and voluntarily superseded justice with mercy. His sole desire was that man should achieve the happiness which was the end for which he was created, and which he alone of all creatures was capable of achieving, since mankind possessed such stock of inherent grace as, by improvement, was capable of winning felicity.

THE CURSE. As a consequence following upon the breaking of the first covenant, God's curse proceeds from him as judge, inflicting all sorts of sorrows on man for his sin, and for his inability to fulfill the Law, principally in the form of death, now and hereafter.

DIVINE LIGHT. The illumination which proceeds directly from God: opposed to Light of Nature.

EFFICIENT CAUSE. A cause which brings about something external to itself: distinguished from *material* and *formal cause* by being external to that which it causes, and from the *end* or *final cause* in being that by which something is made or done, and not merely that for the sake of which it is made or done.

ELECTION. The Calvinistic doctrine of election was incorporated into all Puritan philosophy. During the seventeenth century in New England the Covenant of Grace, however, was the part of Puritan doctrine most thoroughly expounded. But the doctrine of election nevertheless was assumed to be an integral part of Puritan theology at all points, and was expounded as follows: When mankind forfeited salvation by breaking the terms of the Covenant of Works, men had no reason to expect mercy from God in the punishment to which they were doomed. But from the beginning God had purposed to bring back a certain number of fallen men, and provided the New Covenant Way to do it. He had originally appointed a select body of the fallen to eternal happiness, and had peremptorily resolved on the means to effect it. This decree or act of predestination God established before he created the world, determined solely to manifest His glory in the eternal state of men. The doctrine was assumed to be ungrateful to no man that had been converted, and election was most precious to all who sincerely believed themselves to be chosen. It was the sign of an unconverted man not to love the doctrine. By the terms of the Covenant of Grace, God assured salvation to all who fulfilled the imposed condition of faith. Hence the emphasis, among covenant professors, was felt to be rather upon the ability of all to be saved than upon God's predetermined election of a select few. None the less, men were never allowed to lose sight of the fact that God's grace would have been wonderfully manifested had He saved but one of Adam's posterity. Yet He did infinitely more by extending the restitution to a multitude. Though no man could tell how many would share the gracious privilege of salvation (since God reserved it as a secret to be known by men only upon the day of doom), yet men were given to understand that there would be a very great congregation of the elect. Election was no act of mercy. It was not a reward for man's goodness. On the other hand, reprobation was no act of justice in punishing men for sin. Election was never taught as depending upon God's foresight of good or evil in man. The last end of God's election was the manifestation and exaltation of the glory of His Grace. Furthermore, Christ did not purchase election for men either by His active or passive obedience. He merited men's salvation. He thereby redeemed men from the curse of the law, and satisfied justice for men's offences.

FAITH. Faith in God was conceived as the great duty of the first commandment, and was thus written in the law of nature. Fallen men have natural convictions of faith as a duty. But to believe in Christ, and rest in God for life and salvation on the score of Christ's righteousness, under a deep sense that men have none of their own; and to depend on a promise in so doing:—this was the first principle of Puritan theology. To experience faith, the intellect must accept and the will must actively consent to the doctrine. Faith and reason were both necessary to an understanding of God's will, for reason was also of God. But faith was above reason.

FIGURE, *see* Type.

FREE WILL. In covenant theology free will was expounded not only as the power to make choices between reasonable ("eligible") and unreasonable ("ineligible") acts, but as a necessary concomitant of any means toward faith. Since God treated men as reasonable creatures, He expected them to exert their will to make choices.

GRACE. After man broke the terms of the first covenant, Adam's children became apostates, and only by the grace of God, established by the terms of the New Covenant, could man achieve the happiness of salvation. God's Word, which is the Scripture of both the Old and the New Testament, was simply God's making His mind known to His creature, and grace is the only means by which man can recover the happiness which was forfeited under the terms of the broken compact. The achievement is possible only through God's sovereign pleasure, by believing in Christ's willing sacrifice. It will not act by a sudden illumination from within, but is developed by a slow invigoration of such stock of grace as was originally planted in man's soul. It is manifested by God's selecting decree. Inherent Grace is simply the original implantation; by improvement it is capable of winning men salvation.

HAPPINESS. There is no happiness for man except in the enjoyment of God and there is no way to enjoy Him except by glorifying Him. All else is vanity and a missing the end for which God designed the world.

INHERENT GRACE. That implantation of grace with which all men are born and which by improvement is capable of winning men salvation; *see* Grace.

JUSTICE. One of God's attributes *(q.v.)*; His requital of desert; His assignment of merited reward or punishment.

JUSTIFICATION. Man was justified before the law because Christ merited his salvation, and in this sense the term is equivalent to the forgiveness of sins. Man's conduct thereafter, if proper, was called his sanctification, because at the moment of justification regenerate man received by way of the Holy Ghost the power to lead a sanctified course. Justification does not make the offender righteous, but treats him as if he were righteous. It pardons the offender from the accusation of the law; also called Reversion: *see* Regeneration.

LAW, THE. The Law is understood to mean the terms of the first covenant, the Covenant of Works, wherein God gave men a law as a means of regulation, the ten commandments. He made man a reasonable creature to enjoy the freedom thereby gained. Under the terms of the first covenant God voluntarily established an obligation on His part to fulfill the terms of the compact by rule. But man broke the terms by transgressing the law, and thus fell under the curse, from which he was redeemed only by Christ's willing sacrifice under the terms of the New Covenant.

LAW OF NATURE. The unwritten law, depending upon an instinct of the human race, wherein man's universal conscience, or heart, or common sense teaches him what is his duty. It is also extended to mean the law incorporated in the universe through which nature operates, and behind which God as Creator executes His divine providence. It came by the Puritans to be synonymous with moral law, because it was fitted to man's nature, and the reasons for its existence can always be read in the light of nature. The substance of the covenant was the moral law, considered as a bond between man and God, imposed by God and accepted by man. Man as a moral agent was deemed fit to have a moral law by which to govern himself, for otherwise his existence would be vain and serve no end.

LAW POSITIVE. Law which owes its force to human sanctions, as distinguished from divine law; a particular, local, or temporary enactment of the universal law of nature.

LIBERTY. All of God's works are contingent, or acts of liberty. They received their being by a word of command from Him. Man is free in a natural sense, and within the framework of the law. But God alone is absolutely free. Man's end is to strive for happiness, not freedom, for freedom is a divine attribute, in its wider sense.

LIGHT OF NATURE. The capacity which belongs to man of discovering some of the truths of religion without the aid of revelation: opposed to Divine Light. Man by his fall forfeited his original endowment of light of nature, so that even though man carried with him any "remains of God's image", (the vestiges of the light of nature), he possessed them in vain.

LIGHT OF REASON. The same as Natural Reason.

MAN, INWARD. The faculties within, such as imagination, fancy, cogitation, memory, affections (emotions).

MAN, OUTWARD. The faculties without, such as the five senses.

MEDIATION. The mediation was the act of Christ's appearing before his Father as advocate and sponsor for mankind. By making full satisfaction to justice by fulfilling the law, he purchased eternal salvation for men.

MERCY. By the terms of the Covenant of Grace, instituted and voluntarily entered into by God, His mercy takes precedence over His justice. This important consideration sets covenant theology apart from strictly Calvinistic, for it stresses salvation through faith in Christ for all who believe in Him, rather than election by God's pre-ordaining; *see* also Attributes.

MERIT. Merit is what a man earns by fulfilling the law. Even the elect in the Covenant of Grace do not merit anything, but are saved by their faith, the merit of Christ's sacrifice being imputed to them for righteousness. The covenant merit was also sometimes understood as the wage exacted for sin according to the terms of the first covenant, which man broke. According to those terms the condition of forfeiture was disobedience, and the punishment was death. The word is also used in its more customary sense of that which deserves consideration or reward.

MORAL LAW. That portion of the Old Testament law which relates to moral principles, especially the ten commandments. It came to be used almost synonymously with Law of Nature.

MORAL OBLIGATION. It became a moral obligation for natural man to aspire toward moral perfection under the terms om the Covenant of Grace, that is, of fulfilling the law, even though he is incapable of complete obedience.

MORAL PERFECTIONS. Moral perfections, existing only in God, are mercy and justice; *see* Attributes.

NATURAL GOODNESS. Man is saved by God's mere good pleasure and His natural goodness. Salvation of men is not necessary to God or obligatory on His part. It is effected according to His good pleasure, and results from His good will.

NATURAL MAN. Unregenerate humanity, by nature blind and foolish, in whom Satan and sin reign by way of carnality, (evil) suggestion, violence, and darkness. The term applies also to the fallen human nature inherited from Adam, and operative in the regenerate, though not in the same manner or degree as in the unregenerate. In his primitive state man stood a probationer for felicity, and was actually neither happy nor miserable, till by his own act he determined the case against himself. But Christ merited salvation for mankind, thereby satisfying justice, and God then instituted the New Covenant.

NATURAL REASON. According to Calvin, man was originally endowed with an inherent capacity to know God, but his ignorance and wickedness deprived him of that power. In covenant theology, on the other hand, a distinct validity was asserted for natural reason; one in which man was under obligation to aspire toward moral perfection; *see* Reason.

NEGATIVE RIGHTEOUSNESS. Generally termed passive righteousness. Protestant theologians followed Luther in distinguishing between *active* and *passive* righteousness, the former consisting of doing what is right because it is right, the latter in accepting for Christ's sake by faith the free gift of righteousness.

NEW COVENANT. The Covenant of Grace.

NEW MAN. The regenerate nature obtained through union with Christ; opposed to Old Man.

OLD MAN. The same as Natural Man.

ORDINANCES. The rites or practices established by God's authority, as baptism and the Lord's Supper. By ordinance also men should read the Bible, search diligently to find the spirit of Christ within them, meditate, pray, and inquire into points of doctrine.

ORIGINAL RIGHTEOUSNESS. The condition of man as made in God's image before the fall.

PREDESTINATION. *See* Election.

PROPERTIES. God's properties were conceived as two-fold: those that are incommunicable, as divinity, eternity; and communicable, as truth, goodness, holiness, righteousness, wisdom, and power.

PROVIDENCE. God having created man, made an end, and this is His providence. It appears in the way in which He manages the affairs of the world; in the wisdom and order of the world; and in the care which He takes of His family.

REASON. To orthodox Puritans the basic heresy inherent in "Arminian" theology within the Anglican church was the exaltation of human reason, and its reconstruction of God in man's image. At the same time, reason was explained as coming directly from God, even as does revelation, and it is a necessary concomitant of faith; sometimes thus called Right Reason.

RECOVERY. Man's spiritual rebirth through belief in Christ: opposed to Apostasy.

REGENERATION. The process by which a radical change takes place in the spirit of an individual, accomplished by the direct action of God's spirit. The ordinance of baptism was sometimes referred to as the sacrament of regeneration. It proceeds in man's spirit by a well defined gradation of eight steps in the following order: conviction of sin; repentance of sin; aversion to sin; contrition for sin; humiliation after sin; reversion to faith, love, hope, and joy (*see* Justification); sanctification; and glorification, a real change of state, whereby man is translated out of a state of misery into a state of felicity which shall be completed in heaven. At the moment of regeneration, man must labor to fulfill the moral law under the guidance of his reason. (*See* p. 22, note 1.)

REMAINS OF GOD'S IMAGE. The same as Light of Nature.

REPROBATION. The act of consigning or the state of being consigned to eternal punishment; *see* Election.

RIGHT REASON. That which recommends itself to enlightened intelligence, some inward intimation for which great respect is felt and which is supposed to be common to the mass of mankind. Man, though he forfeited it by his fall, still had some vestiges left that might be developed; *see* Natural Reason. The term also was extended to mean correct logical deductions from Biblical premises.

SACRAMENTS. In Puritan churches only baptism and the Lord's Supper were acknowledged as sacrament ordinances. (For discussion, *see* the introduction to *Sacramental Meditations*.) Sometimes called the Seals of the Covenant, they were conceived as a means instituted by God, whereby the benefits of redemption, represented by outward signs, are "sealingly" applied to believers. The Tree of Life was considered a sacrament representing constant life for obedience. The Tree of Knowledge was a sacrament representing a threat and witness of death; it was also a test of man's obedience.

SEALS OF THE COVENANT, *see* Sacraments.

SELECTING LOVE, *see* Election.

STATE OF NATURE. Man in a state of sin is unregenerate; *see* Regeneration.

TYPE. A person or thing or event in the Old Testament regarded as figuring, foreshadowing, or betokening a corresponding reality of the new dispensation; a prophetic similitude: as, the paschal lamb is the *type* of Christ (who is the *antitype*).

WORKS OF EFFICIENCY. Those acts or decrees which produce the desired or intended effects.

NOTES TO THIS EDITION

page 11, NOTE 1 John L. Sibley, *Biographical Sketches*, II, 410. All biographical information, unless otherwise stated, is taken from Sibley's account. Full titles of all citations will be found in the bibliography at the end of the volume.

NOTE 2 *See* p. 221. For a more detailed account of the discovery, *see* "The Crow's Nest," *The Colophon*, June, 1939.

NOTE 3 Richard Mather died in 1669. For a notice of the elegy on Increase Mather, *see* p. 223.

page 12, NOTE 1 *Letter-Book*, II, 274.

NOTE 2 Stiles, *Itineraries*, p. 89.

page 13, NOTE 1 *See* p. 222. The declamation has been edited and will be printed in the *Publications of the Colonial Society of Massachusetts*.

NOTE 2 Judd Manuscripts, II, 215.

page 14, NOTE 1 *Letter-Book*, I, 253.

NOTE 2 Meditation Thirty-Three; *see* p. 144.

NOTE 3 For title and description, *see* p. 223.

NOTE 4 In his funeral sermon for Michael Wigglesworth, *A Faithful Man, Described and Rewarded* (Boston, 1705), p. 24.

page 15, NOTE 1 Sewall, *Diary*, III, 389.

NOTE 2 Holograph note in Stile's hand in the margin of a manuscript extract, prepared by Taylor, of Riverius' *Principles*. Yale University Library.

NOTE 3 *Letter-Book*, II, 274.

NOTE 4 *Itineraries*, p. 198. For the inventory and identification of the books in Taylor's library, *see* p. 201.

page 17, NOTE 1 For a list and description of the Scripture texts from which they are drawn, *see* p. 225. Further amplification of the similarities and differences here suggested will be found in *New England Quarterly*, X, 290-322.

NOTE 2 *See* pp. 31, 33, 36, 137, 160, together with accompanying notes.

page 18, NOTE 1 Meditation 30 (second series), stanza four. *See* also in the second series, numbers 7, 11.

NOTE 2 For a description of them, *see* pp. 221-223.

page 19, NOTE 1 Cotton Mather, *Johannes in Eremo* (Boston, 1695), p. 54.

page 22, NOTE 1 For the meaning of the term, *see* REGENERATION in the Glossary. The word, as used by Puritans, kept its Old and New Testament meaning of one consecrated to the service of God. It was not applied doctrinally to the heavenly state of the redeemed.

page 25, NOTE 1 *A Compleat Body of Divinity* (Boston, 1726), p. 9.

page 26, NOTE 1 On the other hand, it should be understood that though the avowed doctrine propounded by Laudian Anglo-Catholics and by Puritans was the same, there were minor differences observed in practice which were significant. It is clear that *A Confession of Faith Owned and consented unto by the Elders and Messengers of the Churches Assembled at Boston in New-England May 12, 1680. Being the second session of that Synod* (Boston, 1680) and the Anglican Thirty-Nine Articles are substantially alike in wording and emphasis; yet the Puritans somewhat bitterly rejected the Eucharistic ritual practiced by followers of Laud: the setting of a permanent communion table at the east end of the chancel, altar-wise, fenced off by a rail, rather than erecting movable boards and trestles in the middle aisle under the reading desk; the receiving of the sacrament by communicants at the altar, kneeling, instead of in their pews, sitting; the celebrating of the rite daily or weekly, rather than monthly. Though it may therefore be said that the followers of Andrewes and Laud laid greater emphasis upon the ritual of communion than did Puritans, and that in practice they approached the Roman *affective* attitude even while repudiating the Roman explanation, still the Puritans were not less deeply concerned with the purpose and effect of the Lord's Supper, or in any way willing to partake of it as a less necessary or affecting experience.

That Taylor subscribed to the Puritan orthodoxy of his day appears not only in the poetry itself, but in the "Publick Records of the Church at Westfield," the early entries of which are made in Taylor's hand. The manuscript volume is deposited in the Westfield Athenaeum, Westfield, Massachusetts. Taylor's entries set forth points of doctrine, evidently taken in outline from some fundamental confession of faith such as the Assembly's Shorter Catechism.

NOTE 2 *A Compleat Body of Divinity in Two Hundred and Fifty Expository Lectures on the Assembly's Shorter Catechism,* Boston, 1726. Fifty pages are given to expounding the theory of the sacraments, and cover material that Willard preached as sermons shortly before his death.

NOTES TO THIS EDITION

page 27, NOTE 1 *Divinity*, p. 834.

NOTE 2 The dispute with the Lutherans over consubstantiation never assumed very formidable proportions. Anglicans and Puritans seemed to feel that Lutherans believed the real bodily presence of Christ co-existed with the elements of the Eucharist, even though the bread and wine retained their own nature. The Lutherans insistently denied such a theory, but other denominations continued their allegation. Actually, the casuistry on both sides is whittled to so fine a point that it never became a serious issue.

page 28, NOTE 1 *Divinity*, pp. 871, 872.

NOTE 2 *Divinity*, pp. 876-879.

page 31, NOTE 1 Thomas Shepard, the first minister of Cambridge, was one of the most widely read of seventeenth-century Puritan divines. His best known work, *The Sincere Convert* (London, 1652), opens with the following passage, which Taylor's "Preface" seems to echo:

... can we, when we behold the stately theater of Heaven and Earth, conclude other, but that the finger, armes, and wisdome of God hath been here, although we see not him that is invisible, and although we know not the time when he began to build? Every creature in Heaven and Earth is a loud preacher of this truth: Who set those candles, those torches of heaven on the table? Who hung out those Lanthorns in heaven to enlighten a dark world? ... Who taught the Birds to build their nests, and the Bees to set up and order their commonwealth? Who sends the Sun post from one end of heaven to the other carrying so many thousand blessings to so many thousands of people and kingdomes? ... There is therefore a power above all created power, which is God. [pp. 4, 5.]

NOTE 2 *Squitchen* is not in the *New English Dictionary*, nor does it appear in any cognate form. Possibly it is a dialect spelling for the obsolete substantive *switching*, a switch or stick.

page 33, NOTE 1 These stanzas, fittingly a prologue to the whole poem, appear in the manuscript at the very end of *Gods Determinations*. It does not seem likely that Taylor would have assigned them such a place had he prepared the verses for the press.

NOTE 2 *Glore* is a coinage of the author's, evidently intended to express some shade of "glory."

page 33, NOTE 3 For all specialized theological terms used throughout Taylor's poetry, the reader is advised to consult the Glossary. Often a line or stanza is obscure without an explanation of the exact application of the meaning.

page 36, NOTE 1 Taylor uses some form of the substantive "reech" very frequently, and always in the sense of "sweet odor," a meaning not recorded in the *New English Dictionary*. The last example of "reek" as perfume is dated 1599.

page 39, NOTE 1 The line is worn away at the bottom of the manuscript page.

NOTE 2 Proverbial: "Set a beggar on horseback, he'll ride to the devil."

page 43, NOTE 1 *Stob* is not in the *New English Dictionary*. Taylor here uses the word in the sense of "stab"; but *see* note 1, p. 108.

page 44, NOTE 1 The nearest recorded form in the *New English Dictionary* is the obsolete adjective *jim (gim)*, meaning spruce, neat, gaily set up. *Cf.* Yankee *jim-dandy*.

NOTE 2 In logic a dichotomy is the division of a whole into two parts. Seventeenth-century Puritans, followers of Ramus rather than Aristotle, held the Platonic doctrine that all classification should be by dichotomy.

page 45, NOTE 1 The term is a coinage of Taylor's. No such phrase as "slobber (slabber) sauce" is recorded in the *New English Dictionary*.

NOTE 2 Both words, which are dialectical, mean to retch, vomit.

page 46, NOTE 1 With this figure compare the title of John Cotton's famous catechism: *Milk for Babes, Drawn out of the Breasts of Both Testaments* (1646).

page 48, NOTE 1 The manuscript reads *shew*.

page 49, NOTE 1 Possibly *dunch*, provincial English, meaning to nudge or displace, as with an elbow.

page 51, NOTE 1 The manuscript reads *Engims*.

page 52, NOTE 1 *Aqua vitae* was the customary name for brandy or any spirituous liquor.

page 53, NOTE 1 Dialectal variant of *sprint*.

page 54, NOTE 1 In law, an *amercement* was a pecuniary penalty inflicted on an offender at the discretion of the court. The fixing of the amount is called "affeerment." Unlike a fine, an amercement is not prescribed by statute.

age 54, NOTE 2 Although this line has the ring of a proverbial expression, it seems to originate with Taylor. His meaning clearly is that the cold of winter must give way before the warmth of spring can approach.

age 54, NOTE 3 A phrase adopted by Taylor from the Scriptures. Balm of Gilead, or Mecca balsam, exudes an agreeable balsamic resin, highly prized in the East as an unguent and cosmetic. *See* Genesis XXXVII: 25.

age 55, NOTE 1 To *fleer* is to mock or jeer at.

age 57, NOTE 1 *Glaver:* provincial English: to flatter, wheedle.
NOTE 2 Probably conycatching, swindling, cheating.

age 65, NOTE 1 Provincial English: to stutter.

age 74, NOTE 1 Proverbial: "Out of the frying-pan into the fire."

age 75, NOTE 1 The line is worn away at the bottom of the manuscript page.

age 76, NOTE 1 Spike or pile.

age 77, NOTE 1 *Propense:* inclined to, prone.

age 82, NOTE 1 In the sense in which *maukin (malkin)* is here used, it is obsolete: either a ragged puppet, or a bundle of rags on the end of a stick, as a mop.

age 86, NOTE 1 The lines at the bottom of the manuscript page have worn away.

age 89, NOTE 1 Obsolete for *cease, leave off.*

age 90, NOTE 1 Obsolete form of *feud,* meaning active ill will.

age 91, NOTE 1 *See* CIVIL RIGHTEOUSNESS in Glossary.

age 92, NOTE 1 Neither *hard-thoughted* nor *black-thoughted* is recorded in the *New English Dictionary.* Taylor's meaning perhaps is this: "Pray to the Saints (who seriously consider how to help men) that they may free you from malicious thoughts toward those who wrong you."

age 107, NOTE 1 (Archaic): Consents or harmony of voices or instruments. The word has a double meaning here, for Taylor undoubtedly had in mind the idea of agreement, concord, correspondence of parts, qualities, or operation as they were applied by theologians to man's relation with God under the covenant.

NOTE 2 *Kit:* miniature violin.

age 108, NOTE 1 *Stob* in the sense used here (and elsewhere in the poems) seems clearly to mean halt, interrupt, or overpower, but that is a meaning not recorded in the *New English Dictionary.* For its use in the sense of "stab," *see* note 1, p. 43.

page 113, NOTE 1 In the "Poetical Works," between "Verses made upon Pop»
Joan" and "The Description of the great Bones," Taylor ha»
incorporated eight poems, in five different metrical pattern»
which bear no relation to any other verses that he compose«
They seem to have been written as a series, for he numbere«
them 1 to 8. They were probably written in the eighties *(se*
note 1, page 117). Five of them have been included here. The»
are examples of Taylor's experimentation with various poeti»
forms. The title of the first, "An Address to the Soul," ha»
been partially obliterated, and is here reconstructed as nearl»
as possible to what the author seems to have intended. Th»
imagery is highly wrought. Evidently Taylor pictures the sou»
first as a "flippering" object—(and the word *flippering* is an»
other of his coinages)—uncertain of its destiny, and urges it t»
decide upon some definite direction in its journey. Next th»
figure shifts, and the soul is imagined as expanding like effe»
vescent spirits confined in a shaken bottle; then it is pictured a»
a spark that sets a house on fire. Both the variety of figures an«
the conception of the spirit's capacity for error are striking.

page 114, NOTE 1 A *whorl* is a small fly-wheel fixed on the spindle of a spinning
wheel to maintain or regulate the speed. The expression *whor*
(whirl, whurl)- pin is not recorded in the *New English Diction*
ary, but seems to mean the cotter or pin by which the whor»
is attached to the spindle.

page 117, NOTE 1 Dialectal spelling for *wedding's*. The rather vague refer»
ences to the death of the children in this touching poem ar»
made clear by the family records as they appear in the *Nev*
England Historical and Genealogical Register, II, 395, and i»
the Judd Manuscripts, Forbes Library, Northampton, Massa»
chusetts, II, 208. According to the records, Taylor's first chil«
was Samuel, born August 27, 1675, who lived to maturity, bu»
died before his father. The second was Elizabeth, born Decem»
ber 27, 1676, who died, Judd thinks, in 1685. James, the thir«
child, was born October 12, 1678, and died after 1700 *(see th«*
introduction, p. 14). Abigail, born August 6, 1681, "die«
young," says Judd. These were the first four of Taylor's four»
teen children, and the only ones to whom the poem coul«
allude. He evidently refers to the deaths of Elizabeth and Abi»
gail. That the poem was written in the eighties seems clea»
partly from its position in the manuscript, and partly becaus«
the emotion suggests that Taylor wrote the poem while his los»
was still poignantly felt.

age 117, NOTE 2 Either a coinage of a type characteristic of Taylor, or a dialectal spelling for "chuckling."

age 121, NOTE 1 This is on the title-page and bears the inscription in Taylor's hand: "Sacramental Meditations for 35 y. from 1682 to 1717. Preparatory Meditations before my Approach to the Lords Supper. Chiefly upon the Doctrin preached upon the Day of administration." The date 1717 is scratched through, and, also in Taylor's hand, 1725 is substituted. Below has been added: "By Revd. Edward Taylor A.M. Attest Ezra Stiles his Grandson, 1786." No text accompanies Meditation One. All meditations except the first are dated, and the dates are given on pp. 226-228.

age 125, NOTE 1 The manuscript reads *guess*. The text used here furnished Taylor with five meditations; numbers 5 and 6 in the first series, numbers 69 and 151 in the second.

age 126, NOTE 1 *Sprindge* is used apparently (as in Meditation Three, second series) to mean "spread out" or "extend over"—a meaning not recorded in the *New English Dictionary*.

age 127, NOTE 1 The *angel* was an English gold coin, issued 1470-1634, showing the archangel Michael slaying the dragon. The pun is driven home. Meditation Five, on the same text, employs very similar figures, but is worked out less felicitously. See *The Reflexion*.

age 131, NOTE 1 The manuscript reads *guss*.

NOTE 2 *Foist:* (obsolete and vulgar) A breaking wind without noise.

NOTE 3 *Shutters:* (now dialectal).

age 133, NOTE 1 The manuscript reads *mikewhite*.

age 137, NOTE 1 (Obsolete) Scare-fire, conflagration.

NOTE 2 Evidently a coined substantive from the obsolete verb "pill," to strip or peel, meaning here one who is threadbare, hence forlorn. *See* the adjective "pilled."

NOTE 3 The *New English Dictionary* gives an example of the word "snick-snarl" in a quotation from Alsop, *Antisozzo* (1675). It is worth noting that the inventory of Taylor's library lists a copy of the volume.

age 139, NOTE 1 *Pipkin:* a small earthen pot with horizontal handle.

NOTE 2 (Obsolete): A term formerly current in the Universities for a certain small quantity of bread or of beer.

age 140, NOTE 1 *Chat:* twig, or little stick.

page 141, NOTE 1 The manuscript reads *Gam-Ut*.

page 142, NOTE 1 The manuscript reads *every*.

page 143, NOTE 1 A *garland* is a sort of bag of network, having the mouth extended by a hoop, used to hold provisions.

page 144, NOTE 1 On this day (July 7, 1689) Taylor's wife Elizabeth died, and evidently the meditation is written in memory of her, though no special notation of it appears in the manuscript, nor does he refer specifically to her in the poem. *See* introduction p. 14.

page 148, NOTE 1 en + ringed.

NOTE 2 This very unusual figure appears to originate with Taylor.

NOTE 3 A by-form of *cringe*.

NOTE 4 No recording in the *New English Dictionary* helps gloss *crickling* precisely. It may be an onomatopœic modification of *crackling*: the crisp skin or rind of roast pork (earliest date 1709).

page 151, NOTE 1 Apples of Sodom, or Dead Sea Apples, said to grow near the traditional site of Sodom; described by Josephus and other early writers as externally of fair appearance, but turning to smoke and ashes when plucked. Figuratively, whatever is vain or fruitless.

page 152, NOTE 1 Used in the sense of small or insignificant.

page 153, NOTE 1 The manuscript reads *he'd*.

page 155, NOTE 1 *Kerf* is obsolete in the sense of a cut, an incision. It also is used by weavers to mean the wool taken off in one passage through the cutter, in a cloth-shearing machine.

page 156, NOTE 1 Used as a noun, *gay* (pl. *gays*) is obsolete: a gaud; anything showily fine or ornamental.

page 157, NOTE 1 Clearly *yawn* here means a husk or chaff, but no such record of its use, or anything near it, appears in the *New English Dictionary*, either alone or in combination with "barley."

NOTE 2 *Barley-brake* was an old game played by six persons, three of each sex, formed into couples. Three contiguous plots of ground were chosen, and one couple, placed in the middle plot, attempted to catch the others as they passed through. The middle plot was called "hell."

NOTE 3 A small piece of enclosed ground.

page 157, NOTE 4 *Course-a-park* (obsolete): the name of a country game in which a girl called out a boy to chase her. The dates recorded in the *New English Dictionary* for its use are 1613-1675.

NOTE 5 *Shittah* or *shittim,* a species of acacia from which the sacred furniture of the tabernacle was made.

page 159, NOTE 1 Musical term for six Psalms.

page 160, NOTE 1 Saint Anthony, the first Christian monk, born in Egypt *circa* 250.

NOTE 2 *Hone* is not in the *New English Dictionary*. It is characteristic of Taylor's coinages that he often manufactures a substantive; in this case from the provincial English verb "hone": to pine, yearn, moan.

NOTE 3 Provincial English: a sieve, especially a fine sieve.

NOTE 4 Perhaps used here to mean a "bakery," but the expression is recorded in the *New English Dictionary* only in the sense of "brothel."

NOTE 5 This peculiarly apt term for a whale does not seem to have existence outside of this meditation.

page 161, NOTE 1 Evidently "lies in a trance."

NOTE 2 That is, Taylor is not sure whether Jonah was cast up at some point on the shore of the Black Sea (Pontus Euxinus), or of the Mediterranean, in the north-east corner in a bay known as Mare Issicus, not far from Tarsus, the point toward which, Taylor states, the captain of Jonah's ship was sailing. In the Bible, the place is a certain unidentified Tarshish.

NOTE 3 A vulgarism meaning sick at the stomach. The verbal form is a coinage of Taylor's.

page 162, NOTE 1 See note 1, page 126. Here the word may mean sprinkle, or moisten.

NOTE 2 See note 1, page 159.

NOTE 3 Hebrew: "world of righteousness."

page 163, NOTE 1 This is perhaps the most felicitous of four meditations which Taylor wrote on the text here chosen. The others, all in the second series, are numbers 31, 32, and 66.

NOTE 2 Theanthropy or theanthropism: the union or combination of the divine and human natures.

page 165, NOTE 1 A name applied to various portions of the central mountain systems of America, as the Cordelleras of Mexico, of Central America, of the United States, and of South America.

NOTE 2 Archaic: to ravel. Here, intertwined.

NOTE 3 Provincial English: The stump of a branch.

NOTE 4 The flower-buds of the clove (Eugenia caryphyllata) are at first of a pale color, gradually becoming green.

NOTE 5 In this and the following stanza Taylor has drawn upon special information for his lists. His library contained two chap books by Nathaniel Crouch. Crouch also wrote a third: *The Surprising Miracles of Nature and Art* (London, 1685), and on pages 200-205 of the volume are listed all of the "curiosities" which Taylor enumerates in the first of the two stanzas. The information is not present in the two volumes named in his library. No clues have yet been found to identify the curiosities left unexplained by this note.

Lake Moeris, opposite the ancient site of Arsinoë or Crocodilopolis, was an artificial lake in Middle Egypt.

The Pensile Orchards: the Hanging Gardens of Babylon.

Psammetichus, an Egyptian ruler of the thirteenth dynasty, built a famous labyrinth.

Archimedes, by means of military engines which he invented, postponed the fall of Syracuse, when it was besieged by Marcellus in 214-212.

Rome's Golden House was the palace Nero built some time after 64 A.D. It enclosed a lake where the Colosseum now stands.

Titus Vespasianus (40-81 A.D.) finished the Colosseum.

The Strassburg clock was an astronomical wonder built by the mathematician Conrad Dasypodius in 1574, fragments of which still remain.

The "Dresden table-sight" may refer to the magnificent collection of Chinese porcelains which Augustus II, elector of Saxony (1670-1733), was making. The so-called "Dresden china" was not exhibited by Böttger until 1710.

page 169, NOTE 1 As a physician, Taylor would of course be acquainted with the names and properties of such herbs and simples as were commonly used during the seventeenth century. He owned a copy of the most widely circulated herbal of the day, Culpeper's *Dispensatory,* and therein are to be found all the vulneraries, purges, and unguents which Taylor designates throughout the

NOTES TO THIS EDITION

page 169, NOTE 1
(continued) poem. Palma Christi is castor oil; goldenrod, Saint John's wort (hypericum perforatum), henbane, fawnbane, devil's bit (scabiosa succisa), dragon (dracontium), chokewort, crosswort (valantia cruciata), ragwort, angelica, and sweetspike, are all purges or vulneraries—unguents for bites, inflammation, ulcers, and sores. But to highten the poetic effect, Taylor has concocted an herbal: "Plastrum Gratiae Dei," "Unguent Apostolorum," and "Herba Trinitatis," intended as figurative examples of a more divine "dispensatory."

page 170, NOTE 1
Evidently Taylor means that his rush candle flames with a light produced by wick, in distinction from that by which the light of God shines. *Ignis lambens* is a Latin coinage of Taylor's: "licking (or running) flame."

NOTE 2
Harle is flax, hemp, etc., as drawn out or hacked; *hards* are inferior flax. These terms show Taylor's recollection, perhaps, of his boyhood in the cloth-making country round about Coventry. See the poem "Huswifry," p. 116.

NOTE 3
The spelling "Maber" does not suggest a clue for identifying the expression.

NOTE 4
Provincial English: aghast, frightened.

page 174, NOTE 1
Earthly.

NOTE 2
Proverbial: "Need makes the old wife trot."

page 175, NOTE 1
Provincial English: flourishing.

page 176, NOTE 1
Epinicion: A song of triumph; in Christian ritual, the sanctus.

page 177, NOTE 1
The phrase, not common in English poetry before the eighteenth century, appears twice in Shakespeare: *Henry V,* IV, iii, 42; and *Romeo and Juliet,* III, v, 10. More significantly perhaps for Taylor is the line from George Herbert's *The Church Militant* (235): "Religion stands on tip-toe in our land,/ Readie to pass to the American strand."

page 179, NOTE 1
Not in the *New English Dictionary*. Possibly used in the sense of, or by error for, "spraddled."

TAYLOR'S LIBRARY

The inventory of Taylor's estate is still to be seen in the Probate Record Office at Northampton, Massachusetts. The estate was inventoried on August 29, 1729, two months after Taylor died in or near his eighty-fifth year. Four pages of the folio manuscript supply an itemized list of Taylor's library, which seems to have consisted of about two hundred and twenty books and tracts, though some are grouped as "about 28 pamphlets," or "a bundle of sermons." The library was valued at £54. 4s. 7d. Neither the pages nor the items in the inventory are numbered, but they run thus: nos. 1-49, p. 7; 50-102, p. 8; 103-148, p. 9; 149-192, p. 10.

Possession of a library in the late seventeenth or early eighteenth century was not uncommon in New England, but it is rare that one so large is encountered in such a remote settlement as Westfield. Even more unusual is the fact that its contents have been carefully itemized. Any library of the day, and especially that of a parson, would be well supplied with volumes of divinity. Taylor's library is notable in that it contained expensive sets, not elsewhere recorded so early in the colonies, such as Joseph Mede's *Works*, Origen's *Homilies*, and *The Magdeburg Centuries*. It is rare too that a colonial minister's library would be so well equipped with such expensive items as Poole's *Synopsis*, Heylyn's *Cosmographie*, Gouldman's *Dictionary*, Jackson's *Annotations*, and Wilson's *Christian Dictionary*.

Two other features of the library give it prominence. It contains nearly forty books that were probably used as school texts. Recently many of the seventeenth century school books have been identified, *See* p. 203, *item* Norton.) but seldom indeed were they known to remain long in the possession of the owner after his schooling was finished. It is clear too that, as a physician, Taylor took pains to have at hand such volumes as would be useful in the practice of medicine. Some eight or ten medical items appear to have been in his possession, and though the Culpeper "dispensatories" (nos. 58 and 147) are not unexpected, such works as those by Galeanus (no. 157) and Hoffman (no. 17) are unusual.

The great number of items in Taylor's possession that were published after 1670 make it apparent that he did not inherit the major

part of his library, or bring it with him from abroad. It is unusually
well stocked with American authors: works by three of the Mathers
and by such other leading ministers as Samuel Willard, John Nor
ton, Nicholas Noyes, and John Wise. Sixteen works by Cotton
Mather, twelve by Increase, and five by Willard rather indicate that
either through gift or by purchase Taylor was very well abreast the
issues of his times. To find something of St. Augustine (no. 5), and
Greenhill (no. 46), in the library of a provincial minister at so early
a date is surprising.

It is clear *(The Letter-Book of Samuel Sewall, Collections of the
Massachusetts Historical Society,* sixth series, I-II 1886-1888.) that
the Judge sent at least twenty volumes to Taylor as gifts between
1701 and 1721. Items 77, 146, 149, 167, 171, and 180, he acquired in
that manner. *(Letter-Book,* I, 253, 374, 413; II, 3, 4, 83, 97. The
items following are found *ibid.,* in the order herein named: II, 52
II, 3, 4; II, 131; I, 396; II, 83; II, 3, 4; II, 83.) In addition, Sewall
records that he sent Taylor the following: Thomas Blowers, *The
Deaths of eminent men,* Boston, 1716; Samuel Cheever, *Gods sover
eign government,* Boston, 1712; William Cooper, *A Sermon con
cerning the laying of the deaths of others to heart,* Boston, 1720;
John Danforth, *The Blackness of sins against light,* Boston, 1710;
Joseph Sewall; *The Character and blessedness of the upright,* Bos
ton, 1717; Peter Thacher, *Christ's forgiveness,* Boston, 1712; and
Nehemiah Walter, *A Discourse,* Boston, 1713.

Evidently after 1721, few books were added, for none appear
which in its first edition was published after that date. If the date of
first publication can reasonably be taken to indicate the period dur
ing which Taylor acquired volumes published in his lifetime, it ap
pears that most of his library was formed between 1685 and 1700.

In view of the fact that poetry seems to have claimed Taylor's in
terest throughout his long life, it is curious that but one volume of
English verse appears in the list. (See no. 95.)

The library was dispersed at his death, and the larger part of it
went to his son-in-law, the Reverend Mr. Isaac Stiles of New Haven.
Thus it descended to Ezra Stiles, later the president of Yale. ("The
whole Library consisted of about 220 Vol. 'prized £52. of which
about 120 Vol. and two thirds the value came to me in Right of my

Mother. [signed] Ezra Stiles," p. 73, in Stiles, Folio MSS. of 1762, in Yale University Library. In the same manuscript is to be found another transcript of Taylor's library (pp. 73-76). It is not so complete as that in the Northampton Probate Record Office, but the items are arranged in the same order as far as they go. The last page seems to be missing. Stiles adds further on: "The greater part of Grandfather's Library descended to me, but did not intirely come into my hands till after the Death of my Father Rev'd Isaac Stiles." Taylor's youngest daughter, Keziah, was Ezra Stiles' mother.

Investigation has brought to light only three items mentioned in the inventory: nos. 48, 111, and 147. The first of these still bears on the fly-leaf the holograph of the author with the notation in Taylor's hand: "Edward Taylor his book/ Ex dono Nathanielis Stephani Authoris in April 1665." By lineal descent it is now owned by Miss Louise P. Wade of Westfield, Massachusetts. The other two are in the possession of Lewis S. Gannett, Esq., of New York City.

KEY TO ABBREVIATIONS

AAS	Catalogue of the Library of the American Antiquarian Society (1834).
Arber	The Term Catalogues, 1668-1709 A.D. (1903-1906).
BM	British Museum Catalogue of Printed Books.
BPL	Boston Public Library.
Evans	Charles Evans, American Bibliography.
HCL	Harvard College Library.
McA	Catalogue of the David Hunter McAlpin Collection of Books pertaining to British History and Theology in the Library of Union Theological Seminary.
LC	Library of Congress.
Morison	Samuel E. Morison, Harvard College in the Seventeenth Century, Cambridge, Mass., 1936.
NYP	New York Public Library.
Norton	Arthur O. Norton, "Harvard Text-Books and Reference Books of the Seventeenth Century," Publications of the Colonial Society of Massachusetts, XXVIII (1935), 361-438.
PUL	Princeton University Library.

Robinson   Charles F. and Robin Robinson, "Three Early Massachusetts Libraries," Publications of the Colonial Society of Massachusetts XXVIII (1935), 107-175.

SGL   Index-Catalogue of the Library of the Surgeon-General's Office, United States Army.

STC   A. W. Pollard and G. R. Redgrave. A Short-title Catalogue of Books Printed in England, Scotland, and Ireland, and of English Books Printed abroad, 1475-1640.

UCL   University of Chicago Library.

Watt   Robert Watt, Bibliotheca Britannica.

YUL   Yale University Library.

Further consulted for school and medical texts that have been identified as in use in this country in the seventeenth century were: Samuel E. Morison, "The Library of George Alcock, Medical Student, 1676," Publications of the Colonial Society of Massachusetts, XXVIII (1935), 350-357; and Samuel E. Morison, The Puritan Pronaos, New York, 1936.

Books starred (*) have been identified in one of the lists mentioned in the preceding paragraph as texts used by students in New England in the seventeenth century.

1 An Old Lattin Commentary on the Bible. fol: 3s.

2 Foxes Martyrology. Vol: 3 fol: £2.10s.
    JOHN FOXE. *Actes and monuments,* 6th ed. London, 1610. 3 vols. fo
    BM. HCL. (Robinson, p. 115.)

3 Sr. Walter Raleigh's history. fol: £1.10s.
    WALTER RALEIGH. *The History of the world.* 1614 and later. fo. BM.
    HCL.

4 Bp: Jewels Apology. fol: 12s.
    JOHN JEWEL. *Apology for the Church of England.* London, 1567 and
    later. fo. BM. HCL.

5 Austini Tomus Nonus operum fol: 18s.
    SAINT AUGUSTINE. *D. Aurelii Augustini Hipponensis Episcopi, omnium operum.* Paris, 1531 and later. 10 vol. fo. BM.

6 Calvini Praelectiones in Danielem fol: 2s.
    JOHN CALVIN. *Praelectiones in librum prophetiarum Danielis.* Geneva, 1571. fo. BPL. (Robinson, p. 116.)

*7 D: Twissi vindicae graciae £1
    WILLIAM TWISSE. *Vindiciae gratiae.* Amsterdam, 1632. fo. HCL. McA.
    (Norton, p. 431; Robinson, p. 116.)

*8 P: Hylens Cosmography fol: £1.10s.
    PETER HEYLYN. *Cosmographie. In four bookes.* London, 1652. fo.
    McA. (Robinson, p. 164; Norton, p. 409.)

 9 Josephus⁵ Antiquities & wars fol: 10s.
    FLAVIUS JOSEPHUS. *The Famous and memorable workes of Josephus.*
    Translated by Thomas Lodge. London, 1602. fo. BM. HCL. (Robin-
    son, p. 115.)

10 Mr. Woodal on Chirurgery fol: 10s.
    JOHN WOODALL. *The Surgion's mate, or a treatise discovering faith-
    fully the due contents of the surgions chest.* London, 1617. fo. BM.

11 Magdeburg: Cent: Vol: 6 fol: £2.5s.
    MATTHIAS FLACIUS, and others. *Centuriae Magdeburgensis, seu his-
    toria ecclesiastica Novi Testamenti.* Basel, 1559-1574. 7 vols. fo. BM.
    The first general history of the Christian Church written from the Prot-
    estant point of view; later published as "The Magdeburg Centuries."

12 Origens homilies Vol. 2. fol: 4s.
    ALEXANDRINUS ORIGEN. *Origenis homiliae duae in cantica canti-
    corum interprete divo Hieronymo.* Paris, 1684. 3 vols. fo. BM.

13 D: Twisse de scientia media fol: 12s.
    WILLIAM TWISSE. *Dissertatio de scientia media tribus libris absoluta.*
    Arnheim, 1639. 4to. McA.

14 Calvin upon the Epistles of Paul fol: 8s.
    JOHN CALVIN. *Sermons vpon the Epistle of S. Paule.* London, 1577.
    4to. McA. (Robinson, p. 117.)

15 Theophilact upon the Evangelists fol: 7s.
    THEOPHYLACTUS, archbishop of Achrida. *In quator Evangelia enarra-
    tiones.* Cologne, 1532, and later translations. fo. BM. (Robinson, p. 154.)

16 Zanchy upon several Epistles fol: 6s.
    GIROLAMO ZANCHI. *Hieronymi Zanchi . . . in d. Pavli apostoli epis-
    tolas ad Philippenses, Colossenses, Thessalonicenses, et duo priora capita
    primae epistolae d. Johannis.* Neustadii Palatinorum, 1601. fo. UCL.

17 Hophman de medicinis officinalibus 4to 8s.
    CASPAR HOFFMAN. *De medicamentis officinalibus.* Paris, 1649. 4to.
    SGL.

*18 Hereboodi Melelemata 4to 8s.
    ADRIAN HEEREBOORD. *Meletemata philosophica.* Nymwegen, 1665.
    4to. BM. AAS. (Norton, p. 408.)

*19 Lancelot 4to: 1st.6d.
    CLAUDE LANCELOT. (Probably some edition of his beginners' Greek
    grammar, translated from the French and known as the Port-Royal
    Grammar, *ca* 1660.) BM.

20 Brightman in Apocalypsis 4to: 5s.
  THOMAS BRIGHTMAN. *Apocalypsis Apocalypseos*. Frankfort, 1609
  4to. BPL. (Robinson, p. 134.)

21 Durham upon Canticles 4to: 4s.
  JAMES DURHAM. *Clavis cantici: or, an exposition of the Song of Solo*
  mon. Edinburgh, 1668. 4to. BM. McA.

22 Weems Christian Synagogue 4to: 4s.
  JOHN WEEMSE. *The Christian synagogue. Wherein is contained the*
  diverse reading, the right counting, translation, and collation of Scrip
  ture with Scripture. London, 1623, 1633. 4to. McA.

23 Cartwright Harmon: Evan: 4to: 2s.
  THOMAS CARTWRIGHT. *Harmonia evangelica*. Amsterdam, 1647
  4to. BM. McA.

24 Schroederi Pharmac: 4to: 4s.
  JOHANN SCHROEDER. *Pharmacopoeia medico-chymica*. Ulm, 1644
  4to. BM. (Morison, p. 354.)

25 Cotton upon the vials 4to: 2s.
  JOHN COTTON. *The Powring ovt of the seven vials*. London, 1642. 4to.
  HCL. McA.

26 Peraeus Commentary upon Matt: 4to: 4s.
  DAVID PAREUS (WAENGLER). *In S. Matthie*. Oxford, 1631. 4to. STC
  (Robinson, p. 123.)

27 Chaunceys Neonomianism 4to: 8s.
  ISAAC CHAUNCY. *Neonomianism unmask'd: or, the ancient Gospe*
  pleaded, against the other, called a new law or gospel. London, 1692
  4to. BPL. McA.

28 Goldmans Dictionary 4s.15d.
  FRANCIS GOULDMAN. *A Copious dictionary in three parts*. London
  1664. (A "comprisal" of the Latin dictionaries of Thomas Thomas, John
  Rider, and Thomas and Philemon Holland.) 4to. BM. LC.

29 Pereus upon Hosea 4to: 1s.6d.
  DAVID PAREUS. *Hoseas propheta commentarius*. Geneva, 1617. 4to
  STC.

30 Hamten: Conf: 4to: £1.6s.
  WILLIAM BARLOW. *The Summe and substance of the conference . .*
  at Hampton Court. London, 1604. 4to. BM. McA.

31 Tenet washt: 4to: 4s.
  JOHN COTTON. *The Bloudy tenent, washed, and made white in th*
  bloud of the Lambe. London, 1647. 4to. HCL. McA.

32 Schiblers Metaphisicks 4to: 2s.
   CHRISTOPH SCHEIBLER. *Metaphysica.* Oxford, 1637. 4to. BM.

33 Dr. Owens Enquiry into Churches 4to: 8s.
   JOHN OWEN. *An Enquiry into the original nature, institution, power, order, and communion of evangelical churches.* London, 1681. 8vo. McA.

34 Dr. Owens True nature of a Gospel Chh 4to: 6s.
   JOHN OWEN. *The True nature of a Gospel Church and its government.* London, 1689. 4to. McA.

35 Spanhemii Disputationes Theologicea 4to: 8s.
   FRIEDRICH SPANHEIM. *Disputationes theologicas miscellaneas.* Leiden, 1640. 4to. BM.

*36 Wendelini Physica naturalis 4to: 5s.
   MARCUS FRIEDRICH WENDELIN. *Contemplationem Physicarum . . . naturalis.* Hanover, 1625. 4to. HCL. (Norton, p. 432.)

*37 Maccovius loci communes 4to: 6s.
   JOANNES MACCOVIUS. *Loci communes theologici.* Amsterdam, 1658. 4to. AAS. (Norton, p. 416.)

38 Baxters key to catholicks 4to: 6s.
   RICHARD BAXTER. *A Key for Catholicks, to open the jugling of the Jesuits.* London, 1659. 2 parts. 4to. BM. McA.

39 An Answer to the Treatise of the cross 4to: 1s.6d.
   LEONARD HUTTEN. *An Answere to a certaine treatise of the crosse in baptisme.* Oxford, 1605. 8vo. McA.

40 Ainsworth upon the pentateuk 8s.
   HENRY AINSWORTH. *Annotations vpon the five bookes of Moses.* London, 1616. 8vo. BM. McA.

*41 Goodwins Roman Antiquities &c 4to: 9s.
   THOMAS GODWYN. *Romanae historiae anthologia.* Oxford, 1614. 4to. (Robinson, p. 159; Norton, p. 407.) Edition of 1623 in AAS; edition of 1631 in McA.

42 babel no Bethel &c 4to: 6s.
   HENRY BURTON. *Babel no Bethel. That is, the church of Rome no true visible church of Christ.* London, 1629. 4to. BM. McA.

43 Prins apology 7c 4to: 8s.
   WILLIAM PRYNNE. *A Brief apologie for all Non-svbscribers . . . of the new engagement.* London, 1650. 8vo. BM. McA.

44 Edwards Gangreena 4to: 2s.6d.
   THOMAS EDWARDS. *Gangraena: or a catelogue and discovery of many*
   of the errours of this time. London, 1645, 1646. 3 parts. 8vo. BM. McA.

45 Dr: Owen de theologia 4to: 5s.
   JOHN OWEN. *Johannis Oweni Celeberrimi theologi* Θεολογουμενα
   Παντοδαπα *sive de natura.* Bremae, 1684. 4to. McA.

46 Greehill upon Ezekiel 4to: Vol: 3 £1.
   WILLIAM GREENHILL. *Exposition of the prophet Ezekiel.* London
   1645-1662. 5 vols. 4to. BM.

47 Burroughs upon Hosea 4to: Vol: 3 £1.6s.
   JEREMIAH BURROUGHS *An Exposition of the prophesie of Hosea*
   London, 1643. 4to. BM. McA.

48 Stephens. calculation &c 4to: 2s.
   NATHANIEL STEPHENS. *A Plain and easie calculation of the name*
   mark, and number of the name of the beast. London, 1656. 4to. McA.

*49 Jeans. Scholastical Divinity 4to: 8s.
   HENRY JEANES. *A Mixture of Scholasticall Divinity.* Oxford, 1656
   4to. AAS. McA. (Norton, p. 411.)

50 Mystical Babylon unveild &c 4to: 3s.
   THEOPHILUS HIGGONS. *Mystical Babylon; or Papal Rome.* London
   1624. 4to. BM.
   SAMUEL PETTO. *The revelation unvailed . . . proving that pagan Rome*
   was not Babylon. London, 1693. 8vo. BM.

51 Prins Antiarminianism 4to: 3s.
   WILLIAM PRYNNE. *Anti-Arminianisme. Or the Church of England*
   Old antithesis to new arminianisme. London, 1630. 4to. HCL. McA.
   (Robinson, p. 134, 135.)

52 Metallogia 4to 2s.
   JOHN WEBSTER. *Metallographia; or, an history of Metalls.* London
   1671. 4to. Watts. (Extracts from Webster in Taylor's hand are among his
   MSS. at Yale.)

53 a number of Election-sermons 4to 9s.

54 The preservative of youth with other sermons 4to 3s.
   COTTON MATHER. *The Young mans preservative.* Boston, 1701. 8vo
   BPL.

*55 Isocrates scripta 4to: 1s.
   ISOCRATES. *Isocrates scripta quae quidam nunc extant.* Basle, 1571. fo
   BM. HCL. (Norton, p. 411.)

56 Polhil against Sherlock 4to: 8s.
   EDWARD POLHILL. *An Answer to the discourse of William Sherlock touching the knowledge of Christ.* London, 1675. 4to. McA. BM.

57 Mella Patrum 4to: 2s.
   ABRAHAM SCULTETUS. *Medulla theologiae patrum.* London, 1603. 4to. BM.

58 Culpepers London-dispensatory 4to: 4s.
   NICHOLAS CULPEPER. *A Physicall directory; or a translation of the London dispensatory.* London, 1649. 4to. BM.

*59 Magirus 4to 1s.
   JOHANNES MAGIRUS. *Physiologiae peripateticae libri sex.* Frankfort, 1610. 4to. HCL. (Norton, p. 147.)

60 Dr: Owen of Evangelical love &c 4to: 3s.
   JOHN OWEN. *A Discourse concerning evangelical love, church peace, and unity.* London, 1672. 4to. McA.

61 Antissozo 4to: 8s.
   VINCENT ALSOP. *Anti-Sozzo sive Sherlocismus enervatus: in vindication of some great truths opposed, and opposition to some great errors maintained by Mr. William Sherlock.* London, 1675. 8vo. McA. BM.

62 Gladvil of witchcraft 1s.6d.
   JOSEPH GLANVILL. *Philosophical considerations touching witches and witchcraft.* London, 1666. 8vo. BM. The fifth edition, London, 1681, was published under the title: *Sadducismus triumphatus.*

63 the fulfilment of the scriptures 1s.
   ROBERT FLEMING, the Elder. *The Fullfilling of the Scriptures held forth in a discovery of the exact accomplishment of the word of God in the works of providence performed.* Rotterdam, 1669. fo. Arber. DNB. (Robinson, p. 169.)

64 a sermon before king James 2d. &c 2s.6d.
   GEORGE HOOPER. *A Sermon preached before the King at Whitehall.* London, 1682. 4to. BM.

65 Mr: Willards truly blessed man 4s.
   SAMUEL WILLARD. *The Truly blessed man: or, the way to be happy here, and for ever.* Boston, 1700. 12mo. MHS. HCL.

*66 Bucan: loci communes 3s.6d.
   WILLIAM BUCAN. *Institutiones theologicae, seu locorum communium Christianae religiones analysis.* Geneva, 1617. sm. 8vo. AAS. BM. (Norton, p. 394; Robinson, p. 130.)

67 fullers word to a yong man 1s.6d.
  FRANCIS FULLER, the Elder. *Words to give the young-man knowledg* *and discretion.* London, 1685. 8vo. BM.

68 Casaubon of Enthusiasm 1s.6d.
  MERIC CASAUBON. *A Treatise concerning enthusiasm.* London, 1655. 8vo. McA. BM.

69 Roman forgerys 2s.
  THOMAS TRAHERNE. *Roman forgeries, or a true account of false records . . . of the church of Rome.* London, 1673. 8vo. BM. (Second edition, 1689, 4to.) Often incorrectly ascribed to Thomas Comber.

70 Owen of the Glory of Christ 3s.6d.
  JOHN OWEN. *Meditations and discourses concerning the glory of Christ.* London, 1691. 8vo. McA.

*71 Kekermans logic 1s.6d.
  BARTHOLOMAUS KECKERMANN. *Systema logicae.* London, 1606. 8vo. YUL. (Norton, p. 413.) This was published in many editions, for it was a favorite college text.

*72 Downams logic 1s.6d.
  GEORGE DOWNAME. *Commentarii in P. Rami . . . Dialecticam, quibus ex classicis quibusque auctoribus praeceptorum Ramoeum perfectio demonstratus.* Frankfort, 1601. 4to. HCL. (Robinson, p. 152.)

73 Polhil of the degrees 6s.
  EDWARD POLHILL. *The Divine will considered in its eternal degrees and holy execution of them.* London, 1673. 16mo. McA.

*74 Eskinis & Demosthenis orationis 1s.
  Aeschinis et Demosthenis orationes duae contrariae. Paris, 1555. 8vo. BM.

75 Zanchy de scripta: sac: 1s.
  HIERONYMUS ZANCHIUS. *Operum theologicorum H.Z.* Heidelberg, 1613. 8 vols. BM. (Possibly one volume from the Works.)

76 D: Cot: Math: Elutheria 2s.
  COTTON MATHER. *Eleutheria; or, an idea of the reformation in England.* Boston, 1698. 8vo. MHS. AAS.

77 Mr: Willards fearing an oath &c 2s.
  SAMUEL WILLARD. *The Fear of a oath; or, some cautions to be used about swearing.* Boston, 1701. 12mo. BPL.

*78 Poetae Minores 1s.
  RALPH WINTERTON. *Poetae minores Graeci.* Cambridge, 1635. 12mo. (Morison, p. 190.)

79 Massachusetts 2s.6d.
  ? *The general laws and liberties of the Massachusetts Colony.* Published
  annually in Cambridge or Boston after 1663.

*80 Vincents explanation 2s.6d.
  THOMAS VINCENT. *An explicatory catechism; or, an explanation of
  the Assemblies Shorter Catechism.* London, 1701. 12mo. BM.

*81 Cadmens Graeco-Phenici 1s.
  WILLIAM CAMDEN. *Institutio Graecae.* London, 1597. 8vo. BPL. AAS.
  (Norton, p. 397; Robinson, p. 153.)

82 Abra intercession for soddam 2s.
  SAMUEL WHITING. *Abrahams humble intercession for Sodom.* Cam-
  bridge, 1666. 8vo. Evans, 111.

83 Baxters sure way of concord 2s.
  RICHARD BAXTER. *The True and only way of concord of all the Chris-
  tian churches.* London, 1680. 8vo. BM. McA.

84 token for Children &c 2s.
  COTTON MATHER. *A Token for the children of New-England.* Boston,
  1700. 12mo. BPL.

85 Val: Max: exemp: 6d.
  VALERIUS MAXIMUS. *Valerii maximi, dictorum, factorumque memo-
  rabilium exempla.* Paris, 1545. 8vo. BM.

*86 Amesii de casibus conscientiae 5s.
  WILLIAM AMES. *De conscientia et ejus jure vel casibus, libri quinque.*
  Amsterdam, 1630. 12mo. BM. HCL. (Norton, p. 384; Robinson, p. 122.)

*87 Smetius 2s.6d.
  HENRICUS SMETIUS. *Prosodia; de syllabarum quantitate, ex veterum
  poetarum auctoritate.* Frankfort-on-Main, 1611. 8vo? AAS.
  HENRICUS SMETIUS. *Prosodia in novam formam digesta.* Amsterdam,
  1648. 12mo. BM. (Robinson, p. 160.)

*88 Sylva Sinonamorum 2s.
  SIMON PELGROM (PELEGROM). *Synonymorum sylva, olim a Simone
  Pelegromo collecta.* London, 1650. 8vo. BPL. AAS. (Norton, p. 423.) An
  English-Latin phrase book.

*89 Burgursdisius
  FRANCO-PETRI BURGERSDIJCK. *Institutionum logicarum libri duo.*
  Cambridge, 1634. 8vo. BM. HCL. has 1647 and later editions.
  FRANCO-PETRI BURGERSDIJCK. *Collegium physicum.* Leyden, 1642.
  12mo. HCL.
  FRANCO-PETRI BERGURSDIJCK. *Idea philosophiae moralis.* Amster-
  dam, 1650. 8vo. JCB. (Norton, pp. 395, 396.)

90 Just commemorations &c 1s.6d.
  COTTON MATHER. *Just commemorations; the death of good men, considered.* Boston, 1715. 12mo. HCL. MHS.

91 Justini Hystoria 1s.6d.
  THOMAS HEARNE. *Justini historiarum.* Oxford, 1705. 8vo. BM.

92 Answer to Charity Mistaken 1s.6d.

93 Systema geographica 6d.
  BARTHOLOMEW KECKERMANN. *Systema geographica.* Hanover, 1612. 12mo. Watt.

94 Philocopas
  JOHN BULWER. *Philocophus; or, the deafe and dumbe mans friend.* London, 1648. 12mo. BM.

95 Mrs bradstreets poems 2s.
  ANNE BRADSTREET. *Several poems compiled with great variety of wit and learning.* Boston, 1678. 8vo. HCL. NYP. This is the second edition of her volume of poetry: The tenth muse. London, 1650.

96 Admirable curiosities 1s.6d.
  NATHANIEL CROUCH. *Admirable curiosities, rarities, and wonders, in England, Scotland and Ireland.* London, 1682. 12mo. LC. PUL.

97 New Englands duty & interest &c 2s.
  NICHOLAS NOYES. *New-Englands duty and interest to be an habitation of justice.* Boston, 1698. 8vo. MHS. HCL.

98 Statius 1s.6d.
  PUBLIUS PAPINIUS STATIUS. During the seventeenth century his works were edited by Gronovius (1653) and Barth (1664).

*99 hebrew institutions & chaldee 1s.6d.
  JOHANN BUXTORF, the Elder. *Epitome radicorm Hebraicarum et Chaldaicarum.* Basle, 1607. 8vo. BM. AAS. (Norton, p. 396.)
  JOHANN BUXTORF, the Elder. *Lexicon Hebraicum et Chaldaicum.* Basle, 1621. 8vo. BM. (This was the beginner's Hebrew grammer in use at Harvard during the seventeenth century.)

100 Math: Mystery of Israels salvation 2s.
  INCREASE MATHER. *The Mystery of Israel's salvation explained and applyed.* London, 1669. 8vo. BPL.

101 diatriba 1s.4d.
  INCREASE MATHER. *Diatriba de signo filii hominis, et de secundo Messiae adventu.* Amsterdam, 1682. 8vo. MHS. BPL.

*102 Philosophia compend: 6d.

> JONATHAN MITCHELL. *Compendium philosophiae naturalis.* This was a manuscript compendium of physics, and based on Alexander Richardson's *Logicians school-master* (1657). That such manuscripts were in circulation, *see* Morison, p. 155 and note.

*103 Tullie Orationes 1s.

> M. TULLII CICERONIS. *Orationum pars prima.* Antwerp, 1567. 8vo. MHS. has a later edition. (Norton, p. 399.)

104 Colman of Mirth 1s.4d.

> BENJAMIN COLMAN. *The Government & improvement of mirth.* Boston, 1707. 8vo. HCL. NYP.

105 the body of death anatomized 2s.

> NEHEMIAH WALTER. *The Body of death anatomized.* Boston, 1707. 12mo. HCL. BPL.

*106 Epitime Calvini Institutionum 1s.6d.

> JOHN CALVIN. *Institutionis Christianae religionis epitome.* London, 1583. 8vo. HCL. has a 1599 edition. (Norton, p. 397; Robinson, p. 117.)

107 Bellarminus Enervatus 4s.

> WILLIAM AMES. *Bellarminus eneruatus.* 3rd ed. Oxford, 1629. 8vo. HCL. (Robinson, p. 122.)

108 the principles of the protestant religion 1s.6d.

> JAMES ALLEN, JOSHUA MOODY, SAMUEL WILLARD, COTTON MATHER. *The Principles of the Protestant religion maintained.* Boston, 1690. 8vo. HCL. (Robinson, p. 172.)

109 Desires, that Joshuas Resolution & 1s.6d.

> JOSEPH SEWALL. *Desires that Joshua's resolution may be revived.* Boston, 1716. 8vo. BPL. MHS.

110 The Life of Sr. Math. Hale 1s.

> GILBERT BURNET. *The Life and death of Sir Matthew Hale, Kt.* London, 1682. 8vo. BM. McA.

111 An Heb. Bible & a Greek Testam: 7s.

> (This may be The Plantin Hebrew Bible, 1573, in possession of Lewis S. Gannett, Esq., of New York City, which bears the inscription on two mid-leaves in Taylor's hand: "Hic liber est meus: et nomen testabitur idem Quodlectu calami pingitur arte mei Edvardus Taylor.")

112 A Greek Testam: 2s.6d.

113 India Christiana 1s.

> COTTON MATHER. *India christiana. A discourse . . . for . . . the American Indians.* Boston, 1721. 8vo. HCL. MHS.

114 Dr: Increase Math: 2 discourses 1s.6d.
INCREASE MATHER. *Two discourses*. Boston, 1716. 12mo. BPL.

115 scripture truth confirm'd & clear'd 2s.
ROBERT FLEMING, the Elder. *Scripture truth confirmed and cleared.*
London, 1678. 8vo. BM.

116 Bonifacius 1s.6d.
COTTON MATHER. *Bonifacius. An essay upon the good*. Boston, 1710.
8vo. HCL. MHS.

117 Ornaments for the Daughters of Zion 1s.
COTTON MATHER. *Ornaments for the daughters of Zion*. Cambridge,
Mass., 1691. 12mo. HCL. MHS.

118 Decennium Luctuosum 1s.
COTTON MATHER. *Decennium luctuosum*. Boston, 1699. 8vo. BPL.
HCL.

119 Nortons Answer to Apollonius 1s.6d.
JOHN NORTON. *Responsio ad totam quaestionum syllogen à clarissimo
viro Domino Guilielmo Apollonio propositam*. London, 1648. 8vo.
HCL. BPL. (Robinson, p. 171.) Sabin, xiii, 423, says: "This is said to be
the first Latin book written in New England, and the rarest of all the
author's works."

120 Math: of witchcraft 1s.
INCREASE MATHER. *Cases of conscience concerning evil spirits per-
sonating men*. London, 1693. 4to. BM. HCL. (Robinson, p. 168.)

*121 Herebood Collegium Ethicum 1s.
ADRIAN HEEREBOORD. *Collegium ethicum*. Leyden, 1660. 8vo. BPL.
(Norton, p. 407; Robinson, p. 163.)

*122 Theocriti Idilia 6d.
THEOCRITUS. Some edition of his Bucolics or Idylls, (Morison, p. 197.)
used as a college text.

123 The Order of the Gospel 1s.
INCREASE MATHER. *The Order of the gospel, professed and practiced*.
Boston, 1700. 12mo. AAS. BPL.

124 Dr: Math: Dissertation 1s.
INCREASE MATHER. *A Disertation concerning the future conversion
of the Jewish nation*. London, 1709. 4to. MHS. BPL.
INCREASE MATHER. *A Dissertation wherein the strange doctrine . . .
to encourage unsanctified persons . . . is examined and confuted*. Boston,
1708. 12mo. AAS. HCL.

*125 Sententia Theognidis 6s.
  JEAN CRESPIN. *Collection of the most ancient Georgic, Bucolic and Gnomic Poets.* Geneva, 1639. 8vo. AAS. HCL. has an earlier edition, with title-page missing. (Norton, p. 401.) A text for students of Greek.

126 Pastoral desires 1s.
  COTTON MATHER. *Pastoral desires.* Boston, 1712. 12mo. BPL.

127 Heaven the best country 1s.
  EDWARD TOMPSON. *Heaven the best country.* Boston, 1712, 1715. 16mo. HCL. BPL.

128 suetonius 1s.
  CAIUS SUETONIUS TRANQUILLUS. *Caius Suetonius. Cum annotationibus diversorum.* Amsterdam, 1630. 8vo. BM.

*129 Tullii officia 1s.6d.
  M. TULLIUS CICERO. *M. Tullii Ciceronis de officiis libri tres.* Amsterdam, 1649. 12mo. BM. (Morison, p. 356.)

130 (Same as 123.)

131 The churches quarrel espous'd 1s.6d.
  JOHN WISE. *The Churches quarrel espoused.* Boston, 2nd ed. 1715. 8vo. MHS.

132 unio reformatim 1s.6d.

133 Johannes in Eremo 2s.
  COTTON MATHER. *Johannes in eremo.* [Lives of several New England ministers of the first generation.] Boston, 1695. 16mo. HCL. (Robinson, p. 170.)

134 Seneca 1s.4d.
  ?THOMAS FARNABY. *Senecae tragoediae.* ed. with notes, London, 1613. 8vo. BM.

135 Horatius 1s.6d.
  ?JOHN BOND. *Quinti Horatii Flacci poemata, cum notis.* London, 1606. 8vo. BM.

*136 Homers Iliads 1s.8d.
  ?GEORGE CHAPMAN. Probably a Chapman edition of Homer, which has the plural title. (Norton, p. 410; Morison, p. 199.)

137 Pillars of salt 1s.4d.
  COTTON MATHER. *Pillars of salt.* Boston, 1699. 8vo. AAS. BPL.

138 The History of the plot 1s.6d.
  RICHARD BLACKMORE. *A True, exact, and impartial history of the horrid and detestable plots and conspiracies . . . [against] . . . King William.* 2nd ed. London, 1697. 8vo. BM.

139 The Redeemed captive returning 1s.6d.
JOHN WILLIAMS. *The Redeemed captive, returning to Zion.* Boston, 1707. 8vo. HCL. MHS.

140 Same as 126.

*141 Clenardi institutiones 1s.
NICOLAUS CLENARDUS. *Nicolai Clenardi Graecae linguae institutiones.* Hanover, 1617. 12mo. HCL. (Norton, p. 400; Morison, p. 194.)

142 Ichabod 1s.
INCREASE MATHER. *Ichabod.* Boston, 1702. 8vo. MHS. AAS.

143 The History of Oliver 1s.
NATHANIEL CROUCH. *The History of Oliver Cromwell.* London, 1692. 8vo. 6th edition, 1728 in is LC.

144 Pearse about death 1s.
EDWARD PEARSE. *The Great concern: or a serious warning to a timely and thorough preparation for death.* 22nd edition, Boston, 1711. 12mo. Evans, 1525.

145 the wars in Ireland 1s.

NATHANIEL CROUCH. *The Wars in England, Scotland, and Ireland.* London, 1684. 12mo. PUL.

146 Christs forgiveness 1s.
PETER THACHER. *Christ's forgiveness of true Christians, is a preceptive pattern of Christian fraternal forgiveness.* Boston, 1712. 12mo. BPL.

147 Culpepers new method 2s.
NICHOLAS CULPEPER. tr., Partliz's, *A new method of physick.* London, 1654. 8vo. BM. (In the possession of Lewis S. Gannett, Esq., of New York City, is a copy of Culpeper's *Medicaments for the Poor; or, Physick For the Common People,* London, 1670, with Taylor's autograph on the fly-leaf.)

148 old Rhetorick 6d.

149 Hirsts remains 1s.6d.
RICHARD COLMAN. *A Funeral sermon preached upon the death of G. Hirst . . . to which is added, an extract from the private writings of Mr. Hirst.* London, 1717. 8vo. BM.

150 Dr: I Math: upon the sabbath 1s.4d.
INCREASE MATHER. *Meditations on the sanctification of the Lord's Day.* Boston, 1712. 12mo. BPL.

151 extraordinary adventures 1s.6d.
NATHANIEL CROUCH. *The Extraordinary adventures and discoveries of several famous men.* London, 1685. 12mo. PUL.

152 Mitchels life 1s.8d.
  COTTON MATHER. *Ecclesiastes. The life of the reverend & excellent Jonathan Mitchel; a pastor of the church, and a glory of the colledge, in Cambridge, New-England.* Boston, 1697. 8vo. HCL. (Robinson, p. 172.)

153 a bundle of sermons 1s.6d.

154 The singular happiness of rulers &c 2s.
  JOSEPH BELCHER. *The Singular happiness of such heads or rulers.* Boston, 1701. 8vo. BPL.

155 Farnabys retorick 1s.6d.
  THOMAS FARNABY. *Index rhetoricus.* London, 1625. 8vo. BM.

156 a Catalogue of damnable opinions &c 1s.8d.

157 Galeanus 1s.6d.
  ? JOSEPHUS GALEANUS. *Epistola medica, in quae tum de epidemica febre . . . agitur.* Palermo, 1648. 4to. BM.

158 Eliots life 1s.4d.
  COTTON MATHER. *The Life and death of the renown'd Mr. John Eliot.* Boston, 1691. 8vo. BPL. AAS.

159 Guthbeletts logic 2s.
  HENDRICK GUTBERLETH. *Pathologia, hoc est doctrina de humanis affectibus, physice et ethice.* Nassau, 1615. 8vo. BM.

*160 Maccovius distinctiones 1s.
  JOHANNES MACCOVIUS (MAKOWSKI). *Distinctiones et regulae theologicae ac philosophicae.* Franeker, 1653. 8vo. MHS. (Norton, p. 416.)

161 Dr: Math: upon Comets 1s.8d.
  INCREASE MATHER. *Kometographia. Or, a discourse concerning comets.* Boston, 1683. 8vo. HCL.

162 solomons prescription 1s.
  MATTHEW MEAD. *Solomons prescription for the removal of the pestilence; or, the discovery of the plagve of our hearts, in order to the healing of that in our flesh.* London, 1665. 4to. McA.

163 lyburns Arithetick 2s.
  WILLIAM LEYBOURN. *Arithmetick, vulgar, decimal, and instrumental.* London, 1657. 8vo. BM.

164 a Call to the rising generation 1s.8d.
  INCREASE MATHER. *Pray for the rising generation.* Cambridge, Mass., 1678. 8vo. BPL.

165 fuller of faith & repentance 1s.8d.
  FRANCIS FULLER, the Elder. *A Treatise of faith and repentance.* London, 1685. 8vo. BM.

166 3 Dialogues 2s.6d.
THOMAS HICKS. *Three dialogues betwixt a Quaker and a Christian.* London, 1675. 8vo. BM.

167 secret prayer inculcated &c &c 2s.
JOHN WHITE. *Secret prayer inculcated and incouraged.* Boston, 1719. Evans, 2086.

168 2 Journeys to Jerusalem 1s.6d.
NATHANIEL CROUCH. *Two journeys to Jerusalem.* London, 1684. 12mo. PUL.

169 expectanda 1s.
COTTON MATHER. *Expectanda: or things to be looked for.* Cambridge, Mass., 1691. 12mo. (Robinson, p. 173.)

*170 strongs Spelling book 1s.
NATHANIEL STRONG. *England's perfect school-master; or, directions for exact spelling, reading, and writing.* 8th ed. London, 1699. 12mo. BM.

171 Corderius 1s.8d.
COTTON MATHER. *Corderius Americanus. An essay upon the good education of children.* Boston, 1708. 8vo. HCL. NYP.

*172 Cato's Distick 1s.
DIONYSIUS CATO. *Distichia de moribus.* (The book, used by beginners for construing and parsing Latin, was a collection of maxims; it went through countless editions.)

173 Haughton upon the Rise of Anti-christ &c 1s.
EDWARD HAUGHTON. *The Rise, growth and fall of Antichrist.* London, 1652. 8vo. BM.

174 the tryumph of Mercy 2s.6d.
SAMUEL LEE. *Eleothriambos; or, the triumph of mercy in the chariot of praise.* London, 1677. 8vo. McA.

175 the Mourners Cordial 1s.6d.
SAMUEL WILLARD. *The Mourners cordial against excessive sorrow discovering what grounds of hope Gods people have concerning their dead friends.* Boston, 1691. 8vo. MHS. BPL.

176 Yates Model of Divinity 1s.6d.
JOHN YATES. *A Modell of divinitie catechistically composed.* London, 1622. 4to. McA. (Robinson, p. 150.)

177 a Call to delaying sinners by Doolittle 1s.4d.
THOMAS DOOLITTLE. *A Call to delaying sinners.* Edinburgh, 1703. 8vo. BM.

178 Willard of the Christian exercise 2s.
   SAMUEL WILLARD. *The Christians exercise by satans temptations.* Boston, 1701. 8vo. BPL.

179 Angelo-graphia 1s.6d.
   INCREASE MATHER. *Angelographia, or a discourse concerning the nature and power of the holy angels.* Boston, 1696. 8vo. AAS. BPL.

180 sacramental Meditations 2s.6d.
   SAMUEL WILLARD. *Some brief sacramental meditations, preparatory for communion at the great ordinance.* Boston, 1711. 8vo. NYP.

181 Meditations upon the Glory of the &c 1s.8d.
   INCREASE MATHER. *Meditations on the glory of the heavenly world.* Boston, 1711. 16mo. BPL.
   INCREASE MATHER. *Meditations on the glory of the Lord Jesus Christ.* Boston, 1705. 12mo. AAS.

182 New-England platform 1s.6d.
   CAMBRIDGE SYNOD, 1648. *A Platform of church discipline gathered ovt of the word of God.* Cambridge, 1649. Later editions. 4to. AAS. JCB.

183 The fountain open'd 1s.4d.
   SAMUEL WILLARD. *The Fountain opened: or, the great gospel priviledge of having Christ exhibited to sinfull men.* Boston, 1700. 8vo. MHS. HCL.

184 The self Justitiary 1s.
   SAMUEL MATHER. *The Self-justiciary convicted and condemned.* Boston, 1707. 8vo. HCL.

185 Index biblicus 1s.
   LEONARD HOAR. *Index biblicus: or, the historical books of the holy scripture abridged.* London, 1668. Later editions. 8vo. HCL. BPL. (Robinson, p. 161.)

186. About 28 pamphlets 1s.7d.

187 The Synopsis Christicorum Vol 4 £10.
   MATTHEW POOLE. *Synopsis criticorum aliorumque de scripturae interpretum.* 5 vols. Amsterdam, 1669-1676. 4to. BM. This, together with Pearson's *Critici sacri,* was the most learned collection of annotations and treatises on the Bible.

188 Wilsons Christian dictionary £1.10s.
   THOMAS WILSON. *A Christian dictionary.* 2nd ed. London, 1616. 4to. edd. 1655, 1661 in McA.

189 Mr: Arthur Jacksons Annotations Vol 3 £1.5s.
   ARTHUR JACKSON. *Annotations upon Job, the Pslams, Proverbs, Ecclesiastes, and the Song of Solomon.* London, 1658. 4to. BM.

190 Clarks Notes upon the New-Tes: 16s.
SAMUEL CLARKE. *The Old and New Testaments, with annotations and parallel scriptures.* London, 1690. 4to. BM.

191 Dr: Goodwin upon the object & acts &c £1.10s.
THOMAS GOODWIN. *Christ set forth . . . as the . . . object of justifying faith.* London, 1642. 4to. BM.

192 Mr. Joseph Medes Works £2.5s.
JOSEPH MEAD (MEDE). *Works.* London, 1648. 4to. BPL. (Robinson, p. 165.)

A DESCRIPTION OF THE MANUSCRIPT
"POETICAL WORKS"

Taylor willed the larger part of his library to his son-in-law, the Reverend Mr. Isaac Stiles of New Haven. The manuscript "Poetical Works" thereby came into the possession of Taylor's grandson, the Reverend Mr. Ezra Stiles, president of Yale, whose signature appears on the title-page of *Gods Determinations* under the following statement: "This [is] a MS. of the Rev.d Edward Taylor of Westfield, who died there A. D. 1728, or 1729 aetat circa 88, vel supra. Attest Ezra Stiles, His Grandson, 1786." After Stiles' death in 1795, the volume came into the possession of another branch of the family, for below Stiles's signature appears that of Henry Wyllys Taylor, great-grandson of Edward Taylor through the only male line, that of Ezra Stiles's uncle (his mother Keziah's brother), Eldad Taylor. It bears the date 1868. Henry Wyllis Taylor (Yale 1816) presented the volume, together with other Edward Taylor manuscripts, to Yale University in 1883, and it is through the generous permission of the custodians that the poetry is now available.

The manuscript pages, except those on which *Gods Determinations* is written, are unnumbered. The quarto volume runs to four hundred pages, and evidently was bound by the author between leather covers. The items are here arbitrarily numbered in the order in which they appear in the manuscript. All verses, unless the contrary is stated, may be assumed to be written in decasyllabic couplets.

1 A Latin elegy on Charles Chauncy (1592-1671/2), president of Harvard College from 1654 till his death. 20 lines. Title obliterated. Right side of page worn away, hence the verses cannot be completely deciphered. This is one of two short elegies in Latin. Nos. 2 and 7 also honor Chauncy's memory.

2 Another Latin elegy on Chauncy. It is similar to the first and entitled simply "Aliter." 32 lines. This is the second and last of Taylor's Latin poems.

3 "An Elegie vpon the Death of that holy man of God Mr. Sims, late Pastor of the Church of Christ at Charlestown in N. England who departed this life the 4th of February, 1670/1." 66 lines. Zechariah Symmes, born in Canterbury, England, in 1599, emigrated to Charlestown in 1634. He was an overseer of Harvard College when Taylor was an undergraduate.

4 "An Elegie vpon the Death of the Worshipfull Francis Willoughby Esq Deputy Governour of the Massachusetts Colony in N. E. who departed at Charlestown April." 82 lines, thirty-four of which are a triple acrostic spelling "Francis Willoughby." Willoughby, a Boston merchant, afterwards M.P. in England, was an Assistant of Massachusetts Bay.

5 "My last Declamation in the Colledge Hall May. 5. 1671. Where four Declaim'd in the Praise of four Languages [Hebrew, Greek, Latin, and English], and five vpon the five Senses. Those Vpon the Languages Declaim'd in the Languages they treated of: and hence mine ran in English." 212 lines in praise of the power of English as a logical and rhetorical agent, favorably comparing it with the other three more ancient tongues.

6 "An Elegy vpon the Death of that Holy man of God Mr. John Allen, late Pastor of the Church of Christ at Dedham, who departed this Life, August 25, 1671." 64 lines. Allen, or Allin, emigrated to Dedham in 1637. He was an overseer of Harvard College from 1654 till his death, and a man of influence.

7 "An Elogy vpon the Death of the Reverend and Learned Man of God Mr. Charles Chauncey President of Harvard Colledg in N. England who Depart[ed] this Life February 20th, 1671/2, And of his age 80." 86 lines. A series of double and quadruple acrostics on Chauncy's name. *See* Nos. 1 and 2. On the Puritan fondness for acrostics, *see* K. B. Murdock, *Handerchiefs from Paul* (Cambridge, Mass., 1927), liv-lvi.

8   "These for My Dove
       Tender and Onely Love
       Mrs. Elizabeth Fitch
       at her father's house in Norwich"

A very complicated figure in verse: a ring enclosed by a triangle, in the center of which a heart is drawn. At the top a dove is sketched, on the body of which is minutely written:

    "This Dove and Olive Branch to you
    Is both a Post and Emblem too"

Each of the twenty-six lines of the accompanying poem begins with a successive letter of the alphabet. The lines and letters are so arranged that those in the triangle spell out:

    "The ring of love my pleasant heart must bee
    Truely confin'd within the Trinitie";

those in the circle:

    "Lovs Ring I send
    That hath no end"

This emblem is followed by a prose love letter dated Westfield, September 8, 1674, addressed to Elizabeth Fitch as "My Dove." In style it is florid and highly figured rhetorically.

9 "A Funerall Poem vpon the Death of the Hon'd Captain John Mason . . ." of Pequod fame, who died September 18, 1676. 27 septinary couplets, with

the concluding statement: "These made and Sent by Mr. Bradstreet, minister of the Church of Christ at New London to the Captain." Simon Woodbridge (1640-1683), a graduate of Harvard in 1660, was the second son of Governor Simon and Anne Bradstreet.

10 "These for my truely deare, and Endeared Mrs. Elizabeth Fitch mine Onely Love, in Norwich with Care—I had thought that my Muse should have added a Quaver or two vnto your Music but that Stage being so thick a Crowded already, there is scarce any room for it. All therefore that She shall doe, shall be onely to take the tune, where you left it and answer, as it were an Eccho, back again vnto your Song, in this following Ditty." Dated Westfield, October 27, 1674. 64 lines. The verses are highly figured rhetorically, and conclude:

> Thine whilst Mine Own, and yet mine Own whilst thine
> Thou being Mine alone, I'm Thine, and Mine

11 "A Funerall Poem Vpon the Death of my ever Endeared, and Tender Wife Mrs. Elizabeth Taylor, Who fell asleep in Christ the 7th day of July at night about two hours after Sun setting 1689. and in the 39 yeare of her Life." 152 lines. See Meditation Thirty-Three (first series).

12 "An Elegy vpon the Death of that Holy and Reverend Man of God, Mr. Samuel Hooker, Pastor of the Church of Christ at Farmington, and Son to the Famous Mr. Thomas Hooker, (who was Pastor of, and began with the Church of Christ at Hartford on Connecticut in N. England) who slept in Christ, the 6th day of November, about one a Clock in the morning in the 64 year of his age entered vpon. Annoque Dm. 1697." 312 lines. Taylor praises Hooker for his staunch adherence to the older Congregational principles.

13 "An Elogy vpon the Death of My Honoured Sister in Law Mrs. Mehetabel Woodbridge, wife of the Reverend Mr. Timothy Woodbridge. Pastor of the first Church in Hartford, who departed this life December 20th, 1698." 84 lines. She was the sister of Ruth (Wyllys) Taylor, second wife of Edward Taylor.

14 "A funerall Tear dropt vpon the Coffin of [that holy man of] God, Doctor Increase Mather, Teacher of the North Church in Boston and pro tempore President of the Colledg at Cambridge." 86 lines. Mather died August 23, 1723. The opening lines indicate that Taylor knew the Mathers well when he came from England, for he says:

> Nigh Sixty years ago I wept in verse
> When on my Shoulders lay thy Fathers herse.

Richard Mather had been an Overseer of Harvard College at the time of his death, April 22, 1669, while Taylor was an undergraduate, and his grandson Samuel (Increase's nephew) was a classmate of Taylor's.

15 "Verses made vpon Pope Joan." This nearly illegible poem of 110 lines is a bitter indictment of the Church of Rome. Under a form resembling a beast

fable, Taylor portrays the pontiff as an epicene. Though he mentions Pope John VIII (872-882) by name, it is not entirely clear—partly through illegibility of the manuscript—exactly the person he has in mind. It is quite possible he is satirizing the institution, not a man.

16 Title missing. Five stanzas of irregular or "pindaric" verse. *See* p. 113.

17 "Vpon a Spider Catching a Fly." *See* p. 114.

18 "Vpon a Wasp Chilled with Cold." 44 lines.

19 "Huswifery." *See* p. 116.

20 "Another vpon the Same." Two stanzas in the manner and meter of the above.

21 "Vpon Wedlock, and Death of Children." *See* p. 117.

22 "The Ebb and Flow." *See* p. 119.

23 "Vpon the Sweeping Flood, Aug. 13. 14. 1683." Two stanzas in the manner and meter of the above.

24 "The Description of the great Bones Dug vp at Clavarack [near Albany] on the Banks of Hudsons River A. D. 1705. An Account of which is to be seen in the Lond. Phil. Transactions."

    "The Prologue" 108 lines.
    "The Gyant described" 28 lines.
    "The Description thus Proved" 54 lines.
    "His Deeds" (only the title was written) .

In *The Penny Cyclopaedia of the Society for the Diffusion of Useful Knowledge* (1839), Vol. 15, under "Mastodon," is an account of the discovery of these fossil bones, made in 1705, apparently by some Indians. At some time or other news of the discovery came to the ear of Taylor, who became very excited about it, and was convinced that he was looking upon the bones of a giant. Some of the bones and teeth he took to Westfield, and probably reported the discovery to Cotton Mather, for Mather wrote the account of it which appears in the *Philosophical Transactions* of the Royal Society of London, Vol. XXIX (1714), the source from which the *Penny* article is drawn. Taylor's poem was the beginning evidently of what he intended to be an epic on the wonders of nature, and perhaps he felt that here were the bones of one of the giants before the Flood. He compares the bones to those reported of legendary giants, and displays an acquaintance thereby with such characters in folk-literature as Colbrand, Guy of Warwick, the Dun Cow of Dunsmore, and Old Gerion.

Taylor would certainly have been acquainted with the story of Guy of Warwick in his youth in England. (See R. S. Crane, "The Vogue of *Guy of Warwick* from the Close of the Middle Ages to the Romantic Revival," *Publications of the Modern Language Association* n.s. XXIII, 1915, 125-194.)

He would have found it easily available in prose either in the John Shirley account, or in the very popular edition of Samuel Rowland, frequently reprinted throughout the seventeenth century. It was also on sale in Boston as early as 1682 at the bookstore of John Usher. (See Thomas G. Wright, *Literary Culture in Early New England, 1620-1730*, New Haven, 1920, p. 121.)

25 "A Valediction to all the World preparatory for Death, Jan. 3, 1720."
   Song 1. "To the Stars and Sun and Moon and Aire." Seven 6-line stanzas.
   Song 2. No title. Two 6-line stanzas.

26 "My Valediction to all the World preparatory to Death."
   Song 1. Three 6-line stanzas.
   Song 2. Three 6-line stanzas.
   Song 3. "Adjue to the Aire." Eight 6-line stanzas.
   Song 3 [sic]. "Interdiction to the Teraqueous Globe." Three 6-line stanzas, followed by about 100 decasyllabic couplets. (Quite illegible.)
   Song 4. "A Sute to Christ herevpon." 50 lines.
   Song 5. 32 lines.
   Song 6. 34 lines.
   Song 7. 48 lines.
   Song 8. 16 lines.

All these songs, nearly illegible, carelessly constructed and thought out, are written in a very shaky hand—evidently Taylor was nearly eighty—and placed here and there throughout the manuscript to fill up the blank pages.

27 "A Fig for thee Oh! Death." 56 lines. The sole merit of the verse is in the title. His figures are inept repititions of ones that he has earlier used to advantage.

29 "Gods Determinations." For full title and contents, see pp. 29-109.

30 "Sacramental Meditations for 44 years, from 1682 to 1725. Preparatory Meditations before my Approach to the Lords Supper. Chiefly vpon the Doctrin[e] preached vpon the Day of administration." All the "Meditations" are composed of 6-line stanzas, riming *ababcc*, the rime scheme which Taylor adopted for the most part in all his verse. Each meditation is numbered and dated, with a text chosen from a Bible verse. He began the "Meditations" in July 1682, and wrote one approximately every two months through 1720. From 1721 till October 1725, he wrote but eleven. The texts follow the King James version, with occasional help of a Latin, Greek, or Hebrew gloss. It is significant of Taylor's insistence upon the mercy and loving-kindness of Christ that one hundred and twenty-four meditations are based on texts from the New Testament; ninety-seven on texts from the Old, of which seventy-six are from the Song of Solomon, or Canticles, as Taylor always designated the book, interpreted mystically as a symbolic union of Christ and man. (See Quarles' series, in Book III, on texts from Canticles.) Indeed, from 1714 to 1720, and again from 1722 till the last in 1725, Taylor

wrote meditations inspired solely by verses from Canticles. Beginning with chapter five, verse ten, he composed songs on every verse and phrase through chapter seven, verse six—a total of thirty-nine "Meditations." Next to Canticles, the Gospels were his most constant inspiration, in the following order: John, (29); Matthew, (19); Luke, (3); Mark, (1). The other principal texts, in order, were Colossians, (14); 1 Corinthians, (12); Revelations, (9); Isaiah, (8); Hebrews, (7); Philippians, (7). Oddly enough, he turned to the Psalms for inspiration only three times. Occasionally a verse or phrase appealed to him so strongly that he wrote several meditations upon it: such, for instance, as Matthew XXVI:26 (7 times); Canticles V:1, II:1, II:3 (each 5 times). The meditations seldom employ more than twelve stanzas or less than five; the great majority are seven or eight stanzas in length. The longest is 21 stanzas; the shortest, three.

Taylor numbered his "Meditations" in two series. The first is numbered from 1 to 49, and runs from July 23, 1682 to February 26, 1692/3; the second, numbered from 1 to 156, runs from May, 1693 to October, 1725. In the second series he omitted numbers 55, 57, 88, 132, 133. Two he numbered 60. He ran numbers 67, 68, 123, 129-139, 152, and 153 in duplicate. The "Meditations" therefore total 217.

FIRST SERIES

No.	Date	Text	Stanzas	No.	Date	Text	Stanzas
1	July 23, 1682	[none]	3	20	Jan. 9, 1686/7	Phil. II:9	7
2	Nov. 12, 1682	Cant. I:3	5	21	Feb. 13, 1686/7	Phil. II:9	5
3	Feb. 11, 1682/3	Cant. I:3	7	22	June 12, 1687	Phil. II:9	7
	"The Experience"		5	23	Aug. 21, 1687	Cant. IV:8	8
	"The Return"		9	24	Nov. 6, 1687	Eph. II:18	6
4	Apr. 22, 1683	Cant. II:1	11	25	Jan. 22, 1687/8	Eph. V:27	6
	"The Reflexion"		7	26	Mar. 18, 1688	Acts V:31	6
5	Sept. 2, 1683	Cant. II:1	3	27	July 1, 1688	Colos. I:19	8
6	[n.d.]	Cant. II:1	3	28	Sept. 2, 1688	John I:16	5
7	Feb. 10, 1683/4	Ps. XLV:2	3	29	Nov. 11, 1688	John XX:17	7
8	June 8, 1684	John VI:51	6	30	Jan. 6, 1688/9	Colos. I:19	8
9	Sept. 7, 1684	John VI:51	6	31	Feb. 17, 1688/9	1 Cor. III: 21, 22	7
10	Oct. 26, 1684	John VI:55	7	32	Apr. 28, 1689	1 Cor. III:22	7
11	May 31, 1685	Isai. XXV:6	5	33	July 7, 1689	1 Cor. III:22	7
12	July 19, 1685	Isai. LXIII:I	8	34	Nov. 25, 1689	1 Cor. III:22	7
13	Sept. 27, 1685	Colos. II:3	5	35	Jan. 19, 1689/90	1 Cor. III:22	8
14	Nov. 14, 1685	Heb. IV:14	10	36	Mar. 16, 1689/90	1 Cor. III:22	13
15	Jan. 10, 1685/6	[the same poem]		37	May 4, 1690	1 Cor. III: 23	7
16	Mar. 6, 1685/6	Luke VII:16	6	38	July 6, 1690	1 John II:1	7
17	June 13, 1686	Rev. XIX:16	7	39	Nov. 9, 1690	1 John II:1	8
18	Aug. 29, 1686	Isai. LII:14	8	40	Feb. [ ] 1690/1	1 John II:2	11
19	Nov. 14, 1686	Phil. II:9	6	41	May 24, 1691	John XXIV:2	8
				42	Aug. 2, 1691	Rev. III:21	7

No.	Date	Text	Stanzas
43	Nov. 8, 1691	Rev. II:10	7
44	Jan. 17, 1691/2	2 Tim. IV:8	7
45	Apr. 24, 1692	1 Pet. V:4	7
46	July 17, 1692	Rev. III:5	9
47	Oct. 9, 1692	Matt. XXV:21	5
48	Dec. [ ] 1692	Matt. XXV:21	7
49	Feb. 26, 1692/3	Matt. XXV:21	5

SECOND SERIES

No.	Date	Text	Stanzas
1	May [ ] 1693	Colos. II:17	6
2	[n.d.]	Colos. I:15	7
3	Oct. 15, 1693	Rom. V:14	6
4	Dec. 24, 1693	Gal. IV:24	6
5	Mar. 4, 1693/4	Gal. III:16	7
6	May 27, 1694	Isai. XLIX:3	9
7	Aug. 5, 1694	Ps. CV:17	7
8	Oct. 14, 1694	Rom. V:8	7
9	Dec. 16, 1694	Deut. XVIII:15	10
10	Feb. 10, 1694/5	Acts VII:45	9
11	May 19, 1695	Judg. XIII:3	9
12	July 7, 1695	Ezek. XXXVII:24	6
13	Sept. 1, 1695	Ps. LXXII, title	8
14	Nov. 3, 1695	Colos. II:3	8
15	Dec. 12, 1695/6	Matt. II:23	7
16	Mar. 9, 1695/6	Luke I:33	8
17	Aug. 16, 1696	Eph. V:2	9
18	Oct. 18, 1696	Heb. XIII:10	11
19	Dec. 7, 1696	Cant. I:12	6
20	Feb. 7, 1696/7	Heb. IX:11	10
21	May 16, 1697	Colos. II:17	14
22	July 11, 1697	1 Cor. V:7	12
23	Sept. 17, 1697	1 John II:2	13
24	Dec. 25, 1697	John I:14	11
25	Mar. 6, 1698	Num. XXVIII:4,9	9
26	June 26, 1698	Heb. IX: 13, 14	5
27	Sept. 4, 1698	Heb. IX:13, 14	11
28	Dec. 11, 1698	Isai. XXXII:2	6
29	Feb. 5, 1698/9	1 Pet. III:20	8
30	Apr. 9, 1699	Matt. XII:40	13
31	June 4, 1699	John XV:13	8
32	July 30, 1699	John XV:13	11
33	Oct. 1, 1699	John XV:13	7
34	Nov. 26, 1699	Rev. I:5	9
35	Mar. 3, 1699/1700	John XV:5	10
36	May 19, 1700	Colos. I:18	7
37	July 14, 1700	Colos. I:18	6
38	Sept. 22, 1700	Colos. I:18	8
39	Dec. [ ], 1700	Colos. I:18	7
40	[ ] 1701	Colos. I:18	7
41	July 6, 1701	Heb. V:8	8
42	Aug. 31, 1701	Heb. X:5	8
43	Oct. 26, 1701	Rom. IX:5	9
44	Dec. 28, 1701	John I:14	9
45	Feb. 15, 1701/2	Colos. II:3	9
46	May 10, 1702	Colos. III:9	6
47	July 12, 1702	John V:26	6
48	Sept. 13, 1702	Rev. I:8	7
49	Nov. 8, 1702	John I:14	7
50	Dec. 27, 1702	John I:14	8
51	Feb. 14, 1702/3	Eph. I:23	8
52	Apr. 11, 1703	Matt. XXVIII:18	6
53	June 13, 1703	Matt. XXVIII:18	6
54	Aug. 22, 1703	Matt. XXVIII:18	9
56	Oct. 10, 1703	John XV:24	10
58	Dec. 5, 1703	Matt. II:15	21
59	Feb. 6, 1703/4	1 Cor. X:2	6
60	Apr. 16, 1704	John VI:51	8
60	July 30, 1704	1 Cor. X:4	7
61	Sept. 17, 1704	John III:14	7
62	Nov. 19, 1704	Cant. I:12	5
63	Feb. 4, 1704/5	Cant. VI:11	11
64	Apr. 2, 1705	Cant. VI:11	6
65	June 10, 1705	Cant. VI:11	9
66	Aug. 19, 1705	John XV:13	8
67	Oct. 21, 1705	Mal. IV:2	10
68	Dec. 16, 1705	Mal. IV:2	10
67	Feb. 10, 1705/6	Mal. IV:2	12
68	Apr. 28, 1706	Mal. IV:2	6
69	June 30, 1706	Cant. II:1	7
70	Aug. 25, 1706	Colos. II:11, 12	8
71	Oct. 20, 1706	1 Cor. V:8	7
72	Dec. 15, 1706	Mark XVI:19	8
73	Feb. 9, 1706/7	1 Tim. III:16	9
74	Apr. 6, 1707	Phil. III:21	7
75	June 1, 1707	Phil. III:21	10
76	July 27, 1707	Phil. III:21	7
77	Oct. 5, 1707	Zech. IX:11	7
78	Dec. 14, 1707	Zech. IX:11	8
79	Feb. 8, 1707/8	Cant. II:16	12
80	Mar. 6, 1707/8	John VI:53	8
81	May 2, 1708	John VI:53	11

No.	Date	Text	Stanzas
82	June 27, 1708	John VI:53	8
83	Aug. 29, 1708	Cant. V:1	6
84	Oct. 17, 1708	Cant. V:1	8
85	Dec. 26, 1708	Cant. V:1	7
86	Feb. 21, 1708/9	Cant. V:1	7
87	Apr. 17, 1709	John X:10	7
89	June 12, 1709	John X:10	9
90	Aug. 14, 1709	John X:28	11
91	Oct. 2, 1709	Matt. XXIV:27	7
92	Nov. 27, 1709	Matt. XXIV:27	7
93	Jan. 22, 1709/10	John XIV:2	8
94	Mar. 19, 1709/10	John XIV:2	5
95	May 14, 1710	John XIV:2	8
96	July 9, 1710	Cant. I:2	9
97	Sept. 3, 1710	Cant. I:2	9
98	Oct. 29, 1710	Cant. I:2	8
99	Dec. 24, 1710	Isai. XXIV:23	9
100	Feb. 18, 1710/1	Isai. XXIV:23	7
101	Apr. 15, 1711	Isai. XXIV:23	10
102	June 10, 1711	Matt. XXVI:26	7
103	Aug. 12, 1711	Matt. XXVI:26	12
104	Sept. 30, 1711	Matt. XXVI:27	13
105	Dec. 23, 1711	Matt. XXVI:26	8
106	Feb. 17, 1711/2	Matt. XXVI:27	11
107	Apr. 13, 1712	Luke XXII:19	10
108	June 8, 1712	Matt. XXVI:26,27	9
109	Aug. 3, 1712	Matt. XXVI:26	13
110	Oct. 5, 1712	Matt. XXVI:30	9
111	Dec. 7, 1712	1 Cor. X:16	11
112	Feb. 15, 1712/3	2 Cor. V:14	7
113	Apr. 12, 1713	Rev. XXII:16	9
114	Aug. 9, 1713	Rev. XXII:16	10
115	[ ]	Cant. V:10	9
116	Nov. 21, 1713	Cant. V:10	9
117	Jan. 17, 1713/4	Cant. V:10	8
118	Mar. 14, 1713/4	Cant. V:11	9
119	May 9, 1714	Cant. V:12	5
120	June 4, 1714	Cant. V:13	8
121	Nov. 28, 1714	Cant. V:13	7
122	Jan. 30, 1714/5	Cant. V:14	10
123	Apr. 3, 1715	Cant. V:14	4
123	June 1715	Cant. V:15	8
125	Aug. 6, 1715	Cant. V:15	8
126	Oct. 9, 1715	Cant. V:16	9
127	Dec. 4, 1715	Cant. V:16	9
128	Feb. 12, 1715/6	Cant. VI:1	10
129	Mar. 25, 1716	Cant. VI:2	5
130	May 20, 1716	Cant. VI:2	8
131	June 15, 1716	Cant. VI:2	8
132	Sept. 9, 1716	Cant. VI:3	9
133	Nov. 11, 1716	Cant. VI:2	8
134	[ ] 26, 1716	Cant. VI:4	7
135	Jan. 14, 1716/7	Cant. VI:4	8
136	May 6, 1717	Cant. VI:5	8
137	Sept. 14, 1717	Cant. VI:5	6
138	Nov. 25, 1717	Cant. VI:6	13
139	[n.d.]	Cant. VI:7	5
129	Nov. 24, 1717	Cant. VI:7	6
130	Mar. 2, 1718	Cant. VI:8, 9	8
131	May 4, 1718	Cant. VI:9	7
134	July 13, 1718	Cant. VI:10	11
135	Sept. 14, 1718	Cant. VI:11	7
136	Nov. 16, 1718	Cant. VI:12	6
137	Jan. 11, 1718/9	Cant. VI:13	5
138	Mar. 8, 1719	Cant. VI:13	7
139	May 3, 1719	Cant. VII:1	9
140	July 5, 1719	Cant. VII:2	9
141	Sept. 6, 1719	Cant. VII:3	3
142	Oct. 31, 1719	Cant. VII:4	10
143	Dec. 27, 1719	Cant. VII:5	5
144	Feb. [ ] 1719/20	Cant. VII:6	4
145	July 10, 1720	Heb. XI:6	8
146	Sept. 18, 1720	2 Cor. XIII:5	8
147	Nov. 13, 1720	Cant. V:1	5
148	Feb. 5, 1720/1	Cant. II:4	9
149	May 14, 1721	John I:14	13
150	Oct. 27, 1722	Rev. II:17	9
151	Dec. 22, 1722	Cant. II:1	8
152	Feb. 3, 1722/3	Cant. II:3	7
153	Feb. 13, 1723	Cant. II:3	3
152	May 26, 1723	Cant. II:3	8
153	Feb. [ ] 1723	Cant. II:3	5
154	[ ]	Cant. II:3	11
155	Aug. 1723	Cant. II:4	4
156	Oct. 1725	Cant. II:5	5

BIBLIOGRAPHY

TAYLOR MANUSCRIPTS

Chinas Description. This account of China is chiefly taken out of the Letters of Lovis Le Compte Jesuit. [Louis Daniel LeComte, *Memoirs and Observations . . . Made in a Late Journey through the Empire of China*, London, 1697.]. Yale University Library.

Christographia; or, A Discourse to[u]ching Christs Person, Natures, the Personall Vnion of the Natures. Qualifications, and Operations Opened, Confirmed, and Practically improved in Severall Sermons delivered vpon Certain Sacrament Dayes vnto the Church and people of God in Westfield. Yale University Library. [A series of fifteen sermons written in 1701, 1702, 1703; perhaps intended for publication.]

An Extract of the History of the Council of Treves [Trent] which was set forth at large by Pietro Soave Polano [Servita Paolo]. English by Nathaniel Brent, London, 1629. Westfield Athenaeum, Westfield, Massachusetts.

Letter, dated Westfield, September 8, 1674, addressed to Elizabeth Fitch, of Norwich, Connecticut. [The letter was written two months before their marriage; contained in the "Poetical Works."]

Manuscript book. [Copies of a few of the verses in "Poetical Works"]. Yale University Library.

Notebook. [Extracts from William Salmon, PHARMACOPOEIA LONDINENSIS; OR, A NEW LONDON DISPENSATORY, London, 1685.] Yale University Library.

Poetical Works. [The four hundred-page volume includes all the extant poetry that Taylor wrote; compiled between 1671 and 1725.] Yale University Library.

The Publick Records of the Church at Westfield. Together With a briefe account of our proceeding in order to our entrance into that State. Westfield Athenaeum, Westfield, Massachusetts.

Such Things as are Herein contained, are the Principalls of Physick as to the Practicall part thereof in the Knowledge of Diseases and their Cures. being Extracted of of [*sic*] that famous Physi[ci]an Riverius. [Lazare Rivière *or* Riverius, THE PRACTICE OF PHYSICK, London, 1672. Translated into English by Nicholas Culpeper and others, and known as Culpeper's Dispensatory.] Yale University Library.

HIS PRINTED WORKS

"Edward Taylor to Increase Mather", COLLECTIONS OF THE MASSACHUSETTS HISTORICAL SOCIETY, fourth series, VIII (1868), 629-631. A letter written at Mather's request, dated Westfield, March 22, 1682/3, describing a hail storm that occurred July 26, 1682.

"Diary of Edward Taylor," PROCEEDINGS OF THE MASSACHUSETTS HISTORICAL SOCIETY, XVIII (1881), 4-18. The present location of the diary is not known.

SECONDARY WORKS

AMERICAN QUARTERLY REGISTER, THE, X (1841), 384, 401. Biographical data.

BOSTON NEWS-LETTER, THE, August 7-14, 1729. Obituary.

Caulkins, Frances M., HISTORY OF NORWICH, CONNECTICUT, Hartford, 1866.

Dexter, Franklin B., BIOGRAPHICAL SKETCHES OF THE GRADUATES OF YALE COLLEGE, New York, 1885-1911. 5 vols. Volumes 1-3, *passim*.

—————— ed., EXTRACTS FROM THE ITINERARIES AND OTHER MISCELLANIES OF EZRA STILES, New Haven, 1916.

—————— ed., THE LITERARY DIARY OF EZRA STILES, New York, 1901. 3 vols.

Dickinson, James T., GENEALOGIES OF THE LYMANS . . ., Boston, 1865.

Farmer, John, A GENEALOGICAL REGISTER OF THE FIRST SETTLERS OF NEW ENGLAND, Lancaster, Mass., 1829.

Holland, Josiah G., HISTORY OF WESTERN MASSACHUSETTS, Springfield, Mass., 1855. 2 vols.

Holmes, Abiel, THE LIFE OF EZRA STILES, Boston, 1798.

Johnson, Thomas H., "Edward Taylor: A Puritan 'Sacred Poet,' " NEW ENGLAND QUARTERLY, X (1937), 290-322.

Judd Manuscripts, Forbes Library, Northampton, Massachusetts, II, 215. Biographical data.

Lockwood, John H., A SERMON COMMEMORATIVE OF THE TWO-HUNDREDTH ANNIVERSARY OF THE FIRST CONGREGATIONAL CHURCH OF WESTFIELD, Westfield, Mass., 1879.

—————— WESTFIELD AND ITS HISTORIC INFLUENCES, Springfield, Mass., 1922. 2 vols.

Morison, Samuel E., HARVARD COLLEGE IN THE SEVENTEENTH CENTURY, Cambridge, Mass., 1936.

NEW ENGLAND HISTORICAL AND GENEALOGICAL REGISTER, THE II (1848), 395; III (1849), 245; VI (1852), 267; XV (1861), 117; XXXVII (1883), 34.

NEW ENGLAND WEEKLY JOURNAL, THE, July 14, 1729. Obituary.

BIBLIOGRAPHY

Northampton, Town of. Probate Records. "Inventory of the Estate of the Reverend Edward Taylor, Jan. 13, 1729/30."

Savage, James, A GENEALOGICAL DICTIONARY OF THE FIRST SETTLERS OF NEW ENGLAND, Boston, 1860-1862. 4 vols.

Sewall, Samuel, DIARY OF SAMUEL SEWALL, COLLECTIONS OF THE MASSACHUSETTS HISTORICAL SOCIETY, fifth series, V-VII (1894-1896).

———— THE LETTER-BOOK OF SAMUEL SEWALL, COLLECTIONS OF THE MASSACHUSETTS HISTORICAL SOCIETY, sixth series, I-II (1886-1888).

Sibley, John L., BIOGRAPHICAL SKETCHES OF GRADUATES OF HARVARD UNIVERSITY, Cambridge, 1873-1885. 3 vols. (Later volumes are being published.) II, 397-412, 534-536.

Sprague, William B., ANNALS OF THE AMERICAN PULPIT, New York, 1866. 1, 177-181.

Stiles, Ezra. Folio Manuscripts, pp. 73-76. Yale University Library.

Terry, John T., "Religious Influences in American Civilization—Its Founders," JOURNAL OF AMERICAN HISTORY, THE, Meriden, Conn., 1911, pp. 129-135.

———— REV. EDWARD TAYLOR, New York, n.d.

Trumbull, James H., ed., THE PUBLIC RECORDS OF THE COLONY OF CONNECTICUT, Hartford, 1850-1877. 15 vols.

Walworth, Reuben H., HYDE GENEALOGY, Albany, 1864. 2 vols.

Westfield Jubilee. A REPORT OF THE BI-CENTENNIAL CELEBRATION AT WESTFIELD, Westfield, Mass., 1870.

BIBLIOGRAPHICAL POSTSCRIPT

THE POEMS OF EDWARD TAYLOR, edited by Donald E. Stanford (Yale University Press, 1960), is the complete text of Taylor's poetical works. For a listing of critical studies through 1962 see LITERARY HISTORY OF THE UNITED STATES: BIBLIOGRAPHY (Macmillan, 1963, third edition). Annual bibliographical listings of Taylor items may be conveniently found in the March issues of NEW ENGLAND QUARTERLY.

OTHER TITLES IN LITERATURE
AVAILABLE IN PRINCETON AND
PRINCETON/BOLLINGEN PAPERBACKS